HAPPINESS

THE ESSENCE OF YOUR BEING

SHARAM

WITH

SHAHED HARRIS

TALIA

HAPPINESS:
THE ESSENCE OF YOUR BEING
SHARAM

POETRY BY: SHAHED HARRIS

PAPERBACK 1ST EDITION

PUBLISHED IN 2012 BY:

TALIA

TALIA, FRIENDS OF EXISTENCE, INC.
WEBSITE: WWW.TALIAFRIENDS.ORG
EMAIL: TALIA@TALIAFRIENDS.ORG

COVER ART: SHARAM
COVER DESIGN & PAGE LAYOUT: NO MIND DESIGN

"Whatever happens, whatever is here,
is Existence.
We can only understand Existence
when we are not in the mind,
when we are not in the past or the future.
Understanding Existence requires us
to be in the here and now
and whenever we are in the here and now,
we laugh and feel good.
We are happy."

—Sharam

TABLE OF CONTENTS

INTRODUCTION

MELINA: What is your message to the readers of this book?

SHARAM: I believe that our essence is happiness, but many people don't believe this. Most people live in misery, some knowingly and some without even being aware of it. We have to allow our essence, our happiness, to come out. This book is about how to transform misery to happiness. It shows us that to do so we need to change our minds and that if we can change our minds, we can do anything. We usually invest all our time in work and money, with a little, or a lot, of pleasure mixed in. What we should be investing in is ourselves. We should invest in growing, in going higher, and understanding ourselves. We should invest in catching the habits of our minds, or what we call the ego. This book will help with this process.

Ego is all the old conditionings we live by and have carried with us from childhood. These conditionings have been taught to us by society and have been passed down from generation to generation. So they are really ancient conditionings. Mostly these conditionings are about how to be number one, how to win and compete, or how to be acceptable. The result is comparison, jealousy, envy, and overall feeling unfulfilled.

We live according to what we have been taught, but why not live in the moment instead? If we can become available to the moment, life becomes so exciting. If we constantly live according to what we know, life becomes boring. And living in the moment does not mean that you will become irresponsible. Really, if you respond to the moment, you become highly responsible. It seems like it would be the opposite, but it is not. This is hard for our mind to understand because we've been trained by parents and teachers to think that, "We have to do this to get that; we *should* do this, but we *shouldn't* do that; that is wrong; this is right; be still; be quiet; don't laugh or don't cry." The list goes on and on, and meanwhile, we've lost our freedom and are missing our lives.

This book is a small window into Existence. It helps our mind to understand the ways of reality. It helps us to let go into whatever is happening, which amounts to a happier life.

"The amount of richness you have
is not in the kind of car you drive
or the amount of money you have;
the amount of richness you have
is in how much you are in the moment."

—*Sharam*

THE ESSENCE OF YOUR BEING

Master, I just want to know who I am,
I want to feel something solid and not all this doubt.

Feeling solid is doubt.
No wonder you feel so much doubt.

You are a cup without the cup,
The waters of the sea,
The air...no...not even the air,
The gaps between the air,
The vacuum between the stars,
A holding,
But not a holding on too,
Life flows through you,
Not from you.

Let go of the cup
For within the cup
Existence becomes trapped,
And thus stuck, stagnates,
Juiciness evaporating into a sludgy mass
That you want to call "Me."

You already have the
8oz. of sludge
called Shahed
Why don't you try the All,
Instead

"*Having a little bit of fun here and there*
doesn't get us anywhere.
But if a deep understanding comes,
that can get us to a better place.
Yet we sacrifice getting to a higher place
for a little bit of fun here and there."

—*Sharam*

CHECK YOUR FACTS

SHARAM: If we want to emphasize or live by the rules of society and our mind-set is based on the rules of society, we better check to see if the rules of society have produced a good result! ... or is society also messed up? If society has not produced a good result, we'd better double check our understanding of its rules before we blindly follow them.

We have lived for eighty million years and will live another eighty million years. This time around, we have eighty to ninety years *(on Earth)* with this name, this personality. But every lifetime, we make this mistake of living to live and of living by the rules of society. We think eighty years is so long to live, and yet we sacrifice eighty million years of coming and going because we don't want to work on ourselves! We never focus on the here and now and deeper understanding. **We are not here to waste our eighty years.** Deeper understanding is more fun than any kind of living can be! But, instead, we just want to apply the rules of society, because that's what we've been taught.

THE LADDER OF EXISTENCE: UNDERSTANDING, UNDERSTANDING, UNDERSTANDING

SHARAM: All these sittings, readings and books are here because people stick to something. They get attached. They get stuck with something. For example, they have an issue, and they keep thinking about it. This thinking makes a wound in them and creates fear in them. For example, Kate or Maya or Rabia or Tom – something happens for them and they keep thinking about it, worrying about it; they don't let go. So all these sittings happen, so they can open that issue. Basically, this system is created for humans so that they will climb higher on the ladder of Existence – with understanding, understanding, understanding.

CHANGE YOUR WAY OF THINKING

FARIN: You told me that my way of thinking hasn't changed and that this is getting in the way of my growth. What is having the same way of thinking and how do I look at it?

SHARAM: Having the same way of thinking means resisting all the time. It means that when you don't like something, you always won't like it. And even if you change your not liking to liking, it won't make much of a difference. You need to go beyond both. But we usually stay in the same frame of mind or in the same old conditionings. We call this having the same way of thinking. For example, respect is one of your biggest conditionings. If somebody disrespects you, you get so angry. The region you were born and raised in has big issues with respect. Everybody wants to be respected. So this way of thinking has been there for many generations, and now it has been passed down to you. When we stay in this system, we call it staying in an old way of thinking. When I talk about respect, it doesn't mean that you need to change and not want respect. It means that whatever happens, you accept it. When you have total acceptance for whatever is happening, I call this changing the way you think, or changing your conditioning.

FARIN: I was going to ask if changing my way of thinking is possible, but I think you just answered it.

SHARAM: Yes, with acceptance. Instead of getting hurt, you understand that Existence wants what is happening and that there is a reason for everything that happens. I call this a change of mind, or changing your way of thinking.

This is the way of understanding. It is a very strong way—the way of understanding things deeper and using that understanding to accept everything. Then you feel free.

FARIN: Ok, now I understand that I need to accept everything and that I should remember that everything happens for a reason. Let me give you an example. Ardalan gets tough with me and he jumps at me. I know there is a reason for me that he is acting like this. How can I recognize the right reason? The reason could be to accept him as he is, or the reason could be to learn how to come out and to stand up to him. There is contradiction between these two which makes it hard to recognize what the lesson is here.

SHARAM: It doesn't matter if you say something or not, the main lesson here is that you should keep your centeredness. You need to stay centered. You can say something, but with centeredness. I'm not saying that you should act like this right now *(staying centered all the time)*, but this is where you want to go. So pay attention to it. Instead of getting hurt, or even if you get hurt, recognize that your job is not to keep from getting hurt, or saying something or not saying something. Your job is to remember that whatever is happening is a test, or an opportunity, for you to bring a new look to things.

This is a choice, not something that you have been taught. You can look at your conditionings and act differently. Your life will be under the influence of this new look, not that old look that was taught to you. This new look has been chosen with awareness. We call this acceptance. Acceptance means you have decided to program your mind yourself, not to live by the program that you have been given. If you live the old program, you will have a miserable life.

So you see it is not a big deal, but even the fact that you brought this up again after I mentioned changing your way of thinking last time, is out of this desire for respect. When I said those things to you, you thought you had lost your honor; that's why you wanted to open the issue.

FARIN: But I really want to know. I know I have a lot of problems, and I want to work on them.

SHARAM: This is your logic speaking, that you have problems and you want to work on them, but your logic is only two percent of it. The rest is your subconscious, and your subconscious wants to gain respect. But here, even *that* is helping you. You want to regain your respect, so you come and open the issue. You want to regain your honor, but at the same time, you get more understanding. So this is good. You are using it in a right way.

FARIN: Can this respect issue change in me?

SHARAM: Higher understanding helps a lot. It solves all the problems. It's like acid. It dissolves everything.

FARIN: When I see that I'm the same, I feel hopeless and disappointed.

SHARAM: Disappointment happens when there is no understanding. Now that I have opened things and you've gotten understanding, you really don't feel disappointed. You are laughing and you are happy. Understanding brings people out of disappointment. That's why you ask me to open something. Even at the time that you asked me to open this issue, you were smiling. You knew that everything was going to be fine, after we opened it, that we would solve the problem together.

Now, about this situation between you and Ardalan. You need to understand that Ardalan has a temper. This is him. He jumps on everybody who says something that he doesn't like. So it has nothing to do with you. This is him with his temper. You need to give him space to be himself, to live his personality. This is not about Ardalan, it's about you. It's about you understanding that it is not your fault when he jumps on you. It is just his personality, his character. If you have done nothing wrong, then what is the problem with him acting like that? You need to give him space to act like this. Change your way of thinking and see things differently.

Since childhood, we have been taught that if someone jumps on you, you should get hurt, and you are doing exactly what you have been told. But now I'm telling you to change your mind. When you have done nothing wrong to be yelled at, let him yell. Let him do whatever he wants to do. It has nothing to do with you. You just look at him, either smile or smile inside and say, this is Ardalan doing Ardalan-y things. We call this looking differently. But we haven't been taught this.

FARIN: I feel like you have given me new eyes, a new way to look at things.

SHARAM: You have always wanted to be independent. You've always wanted to live your own life, to be independent, and to make your own money. But independence in the traditional sense really wasn't what you were after. What you were after was this. This is the main thing that you wanted, that you have been looking for—to have your own look. To have your own eye.

FARIN: Really, when we look at things differently, everything changes. You do it. You always look at things differently.

SHARAM: I have been told many times that I look at things differently, and I have lots of different stories about it. I just want to tell one of them. Once when I was in Boston, there was this lady who was the manager of a non-profit organization. She liked my way of thinking and she wanted to hire me. While I was working for them, she often said that I looked at things so differently, that's why she hired me. But when it got to the point that I started to see things differently about her ideas too, she didn't like it and she fired me. *(Lots of laughter)* It was funny that she hired me and fired me because I was looking at things differently.

LOVE, CULTURE AND CONDITIONING

STREAM: My son and his Chinese fiancé visited me for a long weekend. My son had come home to relax and recuperate and to have his girl and his Mom get to know each other. For the most part she was a perfect guest. She was observant, thoughtful, considerate, respectful; she was not shy or too timid. She cooked one breakfast and some side dishes at other meals and she helped in the garden.

Nevertheless, two things about her bothered me. First, I thought she treated me like an old person who couldn't take care of herself; but more importantly, she kept fussing and poking at Nick to treat me that way also. Second, I felt she was pushy with him and generally critical of Nick's behavior. For example, he was fixing a bowl of cereal for himself one morning when she came to the kitchen. She asked if it was for her, so he said she could have that bowl and he went to fix another for himself. He asked very simply if she could pour coffee for the two of them. She snapped that he couldn't just do something for her without asking her to do something back. I could see that he felt misunderstood and was hurt, but he didn't argue. My heart hurt for him.

SHARAM: With respect to this woman wanting to do everything for you, she was acting out of love and your reaction was ego!

STREAM: I thought there was simply a cultural difference happening.

SHARAM: Don't put the blame on different cultures, the problem is your ego. *(To the group)* In the West people are raised to be independent, to take care of themselves and be proud of it. Also, Westerners worship youth and so does Stream! She doesn't want someone to suggest that she's not youthful. But the Chinese respect their elders and want to take care of them. They feel that the parents took care of the children for so many years that, once the children are old enough, they should take care of the parents. So, she was not judging you Stream or suggesting that you are not capable or that you are old; rather, she was respecting you. She was also teaching your son to act out of love even though she might be doing it unconsciously.

As far as her criticizing your son or being antagonistic or hostile, she is going to push him towards enlightenment! Her goal in life is to have a job, a home and children; your son is still figuring out what his goal is. She will create suffering for him and that suffering will draw him towards spiritual work.

"Good and bad don't really exist.
Someone just told us,
'This is bad,' and we believed it.
Which is fine, just know that
good and bad are arbitrary.
Someone pulled them out of a hat
and that's the way it's been
for a thousand years."

—Sharam

THE BIGGER PICTURE

SHARAM: When something negative happens, if I only look at it from a smaller point of view, it hurts me, but if I understand the bigger picture, I become happy!

OVERCOMING THE DUALITY OF EARTH

KATE: Am I really that bad?

SHARAM: Yes, you really are that bad. You are also really good. Everybody is like that. If one is good, one is bad too. I have both the Devil and God inside of me. So I am both bad and good. I'm Tea Bag and Michael *(characters on the show Prison Break). Lots of laughter.*

KATE: Do you hate me?

SHARAM: Yes, I hate you; I also love you. When the bad part of you comes out, it brings out the bad part in me, so the two parts start fighting with each other and we hate each other. This is the nature of Existence. Then, when your good side comes out, it brings out my good side and we love each other.

This is the duality of Earth. It is always like this. But there is something else you should know. This is a law of Existence. Everybody has this harsh part. If you didn't have this part, you would not be alive on Earth. Because I know this and accept it, I respect Existence's rules; I don't fall into this cycle. When that harsh part comes out, in my eyes that is not you. It's Existence and I love Existence. You are Existence in this body, with this mind that has been conditioned to be good so others will like you. Because of this conditioning, you don't like your own harsh part. That harsh part doesn't really affect me. I know better.

"All good things come with a bad."

—*Sharam*

"The heart is like a radar.
Every time there's something positive,
it detects it.
The heart doesn't catch the negative,
and the mind doesn't catch the positive."

—*Sharam*

POSITIVE/NEGATIVE
HEART/MIND

SHARAM: Everything that is being said, or everything that is being done—anything—has a negative and a positive. If it doesn't have a negative and a positive, it doesn't work. Even when you talk, the negative and positive have to be there. The mind detects the negative and the heart detects the positive.

Anything that is being said, like "Hello," the mind thinks, "What does he want from me?" while the heart says, "Oh, he's so friendly." Or if someone is quiet, the mind says, "She's so passive," but the heart says, "She's so innocent, so beautiful."

If you are in the mind intensively, that's all you see—negativity: "He's a bully, she's crazy, she's passive," etc., but the heart says, "He's so strong, she lives so much in the moment, she's so innocent, so beautiful."

*"Someone who works with others
is called a spiritual master.
Just like a master of ceremonies,
masterpiece, or master bedroom,
only a spiritual master
is one who is master of the ego."*

—*Sharam*

WHAT WILL PEOPLE THINK?

MONA: How can I put aside my ego and not worry about whether others will like me or not?

SHARAM: Even God likes to be liked. Do you know why? Because whoever loves God will enjoy, and God wants everybody to be happy and have joy in their life. Everything that is given to us is necessary, even ego. We have ego. Then, when the time comes that we don't need ego anymore, it fades away or it all of a sudden drops.

If you have not reached to your own center, you fall into everybody's game or into whatever is around you, and this is good because if you don't, you will not grow. When you enter into your being, nothing can change you. You are in the maximum of ecstasy and bliss. Nothing can add or deduct from your ecstasy. You are in the highest stage all the time, unless you start working with people. Then you have to go to the same level as the individual. A master can travel between the chakras, low and high, easily. For him, it doesn't matter what others think or if they like him or not, because he is already at the maximum of ecstasy. But he too, wants people to like him, because when someone loves the master or God, they will enjoy their life and feel bliss more.

MONA: Sharam, can you give me an example of how a master doesn't care what others think?

SHARAM: One day a man wants to travel, so he goes to the most trust-worthy person in the town and says to him, "I am going off to travel for awhile and since you are the most trustworthy person in town, I want to ask if I can leave my daughter with you until I get back." The trustworthy man says, "Let me think about it for a day and I will let you know." He goes to his master and says, "Master I don't know what to do. This man wants to leave his daughter with me while he travels, but I am in love with her. What should I do?" The master gives him the address of a man in town who is known for having a house of prostitution with young girls and boys, and tells him to go ask that man what he should do. So the trustworthy man goes to the house, hidingly, so no one will see him. When he knocks on the door a beautiful young girl opens it and invites him in. She takes him to a room where the owner of the house is sitting with a beautiful boy and girl sitting on his lap. He offers the trusted man a drink even though he knows his visitor doesn't drink alcohol. "No thank you," says the trusted man. The owner says, "I know why you are here! You love that girl, and her father wants you to watch over her while he is gone. It is for that very reason I create situations where everybody thinks I am a bad man, but I want you to know that these are my children and this is not wine. It is just fruit juice. I do this so that others will not bother us, and we are free to do our meditations uninterrupted."

The trusted man leaves the house with a new understanding. He realizes he has lived his whole life so that people will like him and trust him, and so that he will feel important. After this, the trusted man puts all this aside to focus on his own meditations.

I told you this story since you asked how you can work on your ego and not be dependent on whether people like you or not. Just remember, when you start to worry, say, "Yes this is ego, but it is necessary because it is directing me to real compassion."

*"To have love and compassion for others,
regardless of how they treat you,
you must have an open heart."*

—*Sharam*

MASTER VISITED ME AT THE GYM TODAY

Speaking of exercise,
I was working out today,
Throwing a medicine ball
High against a wall,
Then, catching it
Squatting low,
And throwing it up,
Over and over again.
Until, suddenly, I started to feel
Like a dog chasing my own tail.

"How is it," Master chuckled, in my ear
"That you can do this every day,
But not sit,
Relaxed and breathing for the same amount of time?
Relaxation...or...torture?
Achy joints and knotted muscles...
or,
A relaxed mind and peaceful heart."

Feeling his soft kiss
On my sweaty brow
I totally forget the heavy ball
Spiraling down to smack
My trembling toe.

"Thank you, Master," I smiled,
Limping happily home.

THE THREE COMPONENTS
OF A SUCCESSFUL LIFE

SHARAM: Life is like braiding your hair. The three parts of braiding consist of work, having fun, and meditation. If one of them is not there, life will be meaningless. Exercises and meditation should be woven in-between the other two. Make a schedule to ensure that you take care of all three throughout your day.

THINGS HAVE TO GET WORSE
TO GET BETTER

CHRIS: You asked me why I hide. I don't have any idea why. I can't remember anything that would cause it.

SHARAM: I will tell you a story. I've been working with Nima for twelve years now. His sense of guilt, feeling sorry, and the sorrow he carries—he didn't know where it came from. For twelve years, every time he tried to understand it, he could not. We had sittings and sittings and sittings and classes, and I always would remind him that he is so sad, he is so angry. He did not know where it came from. Finally, yesterday he found out why. He said all of a sudden it came to him.

His brother died, so he felt guilty. He didn't know why he felt guilty. Yesterday he found out. One day he was supposed to go and pick his brother up from school. But on that day, some of his friends got together. Somebody had bought this brand new Ford Mustang. They were cruising down the street really fast and they were having lots of fun. They passed by the school. Nima saw his brother standing there, but he said, "I was too passive to tell my friend to stop, so I could pick up my brother." He just cruised on and went fast. All of a sudden his friend stopped at a place and said, "I really need to go. You need to get out." Nima got out and got a taxi and went to the school, but his brother was gone. He had gone home. Nima felt guilty. He saw his brother, but he was too passive to tell his friend to stop the car so he could pick his brother up.

He still feels guilty many years later. He said, "I never ever remembered this," but finally it came alive for him. His brother didn't die that day, but every time Nima thinks about his brother, he feels guilty. He remembers his brother standing in front of that school waiting for him, and he feels he wasn't caring enough towards his brother. Even though he didn't remember the incident, the feeling of not being caring got stuck with him. Now, he feels regret and guilt.

Your hiding, Chris, is the same thing. There is something behind it. Eventually you will remember. It was such a relief for Nima to remember.

"The ego is not easy to catch because it manipulates us constantly and in very subtle ways."

—*Sharam*

*"Never bother with the thought
'I wish I'd known this earlier.'
We need to understand that
Existence reveals itself to us
in the moment
when we are ready;
when it is the right time."*

—Sharam

DESTROYING OTHERS WITH OUR GUILT

JESSE: I have been thinking about all the times in the past when you were so loving to me and I was so horrible back to you because of my ego.

SHARAM: There is no Existence except you. You are the universe. If you don't forgive yourself, Existence is not forgiving you, because you are Existence.

JESSE: So how can I forgive myself, Sharam?

SHARAM: When you keep doing this *(not forgiving and going to the past)*, you destroy this moment. So not only did you destroy that moment in the past, but you are destroying this moment too. If you don't forgive yourself for what you have done before, you are doing the same thing again without actually doing it. You are throwing the karma of all the past negativities on me.

JESSE: So how can I forgive myself?

SHARAM: Just know this. That you are doing the same thing. You are destroying me. Ok, let's say that Livia doesn't forgive herself for something she has done to Tom, ok? For years and years, every time she sees

Tom, she feels bad about what has happened. Then that negative energy gets directed towards Tom, so she is doing the same thing but very subtly. She is destroying Tom again, because she can't forgive herself for something she has done to Tom. Know this strongly and forgive yourself, because you are really destroying me.

JESSE: Will you forgive me?

SHARAM: I have nothing to do with it.

JESSE: I just feel terrible about how I messed everything up.

SHARAM: You didn't mess anything up. You are messing everything up now. Before you were growing you had a excuse, but right now there is no more excuse. Don't do it. Just don't do it.

DEFENDING OURSELVES:
A SIGN OF GUILT

FARIN: Why do I defend myself so much? Even in a situation that I am not involved in, I find myself defending myself in advance to avoid any accusation.

SHARAM: The other day, Maya said something interesting. She said in certain situations, we defend ourselves so much, acting as if we are saints who can do no wrong. Then we keep asking you, "Sharam, what is my problem?" The problem is so clear. The problem *is* defending yourself. When something happens, deep down you think it is your fault. Deep down you think that all the problems of the world are because of you.

Feeling guilt is something that, since childhood, you have been nourished with, raised with. It is deep in your subconscious. So when a person breaks a glass over there, you feel guilty over here. You might even go to him and start apologizing for a glass that he broke. You start apologizing because deep down, you think that everything is your fault. Then, because you think everything is your fault, you start defending. But you should know that it is not your fault, it is just Existence happening and has nothing to do with you.

FARIN: What can I do with this feeling? It causes me to be on guard all the time instead of open. It seems to be the source of all my worrying and anxiety.

SHARAM: Anytime you start defending yourself, know that this defending is just on the surface; that below this defending is the feeling that something is your fault. Just pay attention to it. We cannot do anything about it. It is just through watching that you can do something about it. We cannot *do* anything about anything. If we have grown thus far, it has happened by watching. When we start paying attention every time something happens, just by paying attention to it, we will go beyond it. So our growth is because of paying attention, even if we are not aware of the mechanism of it.

We have been taught that the outside world and what we show to people on the outside is so important. For example we have learned our homes should be clean. When we are home by ourselves we don't care so much, but if someone comes over, we rush around shoving any mess into our closets, or under the couch. Then when they leave, everything comes out again. We have been taught that the outside is important, that's why we become so showy and stay on the surface. We just want to show that we are good.

Just know that the defending is because of the guilt. On the surface, it manifests itself as the opposite, You defend, proclaiming your innocence, but anyone who is truly innocent won't defend himself. And remember what I said earlier, it is not your fault. If you really deeply feel that you are not at fault, you won't defend yourself.

THE BANKS OF THE RIVER

CHRIS: I've gone from wanting attention to being scared to death of it. I am afraid to look at you. I have a lot of fear.

SHARAM: Good. I am glad you are experiencing the opposite bank of the river. The fear has come to the surface. You can look at it or not. It is an opportunity. Before, you didn't even know that there was another side. Now you know. Before, you were only on the side of the river that wanted attention. You didn't know this side.

CHRIS: It seems I only go to the extremes. I don't have any balance. I don't know how to achieve the balance.

SHARAM: Exactly. The balance only comes when you become enlightened. The balance is never there until one becomes enlightened.

CHRIS: So I should just continue on in class like I am doing now?

SHARAM: Yes, not looking at me, being afraid of looking at me is good, because then you look at your fear. It is an opportunity. The fear has come to the surface. If you look at it, it will go away. If you don't look at it, it goes back in. Existence, no matter how negative or positive you are, is all about love, and love is beyond positive or negative. So whatever happens to you is pure love. It is pointing out something to you, helping you to grow. It is pushing you away from somewhere that you are stuck. It is all amazing. Love is beyond negative and positive. It is an opportunity to look at yourself.

CHRIS: Going through this, I don't feel any heart, which I feel is part of the reason I am so worried about it.

SHARAM: Everything has a cost, and the cost of being fearful and looking at your fear is the fact that you don't go to your heart. You still go a little bit; when I say good night, when I am leaving, I see that you do go to your heart.

CONDEMNING OURSELVES AND OTHERS

SHARAM: Something happened last night which was very interesting. We were watching a show and Baba made a comment that Chris didn't like. Then, we opened the issue. I told Chris, "See how much you don't like? When you don't like something, you push Existence away for your own selfishness." It's all about the self. It is about the ego and protecting the ego. The only thing in us that gets hurt is the ego, and yet we want to protect it.

CHRIS: I stuff it and stuff it and stuff it; and then when I say something, it just exposes how horrible I am. Then, I just want to give up.

SHARAM: There is a rejection of who you are. That is the real problem. So something comes up, but because you reject who you are, you don't want to look at it. Then a half hour later, this mood passes, but meanwhile you missed looking at it because of this rejection. Rejection means putting a curtain up between ourselves and this thing about ourselves that we don't like. We walk away and never look at ourselves because the curtain is there. That rejection of the self is the reason we can't see this thing about ourselves. Again and again it comes up and again and again we reject it, and we keep missing the opportunity to look.

A different route would be to not reject it, but to accept. How do we accept? By saying, "Look, my issue is so tiny, so small." We could say the same thing in a rejecting way: "Look at me, I'm so stupid. This tiny thing, I don't get it. It's always the same." Now the positive way is: "My issue is so tiny. I don't have much of a problem. It is such a blessing."

CHRIS: But, my issue is terrible. It affects everybody. It isn't tiny.

SHARAM: Again you are looking at it from the negative angle. *"It affects everybody."*

CHRIS: But it *does.*

SHARAM: It doesn't matter. It is tiny. You can fix it. Look at it without judgment, without condemning it, because condemnation puts up this curtain, this big wall and we can't see the issue directly. For once, let's just look at it a different way.

CHRIS: I don't accept anybody or anything. How is that tiny?

SHARAM: It *is* tiny. Think of people who owe half a million dollars and they are in jail. They have huge issues. When you talk to someone from a third world country and you say you are worried about these things, they say, "Come on, we are starving to death and you are worried about this tiny thing. People are after me to put me in jail. I owe them. I am starving. My wife is dying from sickness. I can't afford anything. You guys are nuts, worrying about not accepting." So it is nothing. It is tiny. It is little. If we make it like a monster, we are afraid of it. We make it huge again. It is not. It is just a tiny thing. People are not after you to put you in jail. You are not starving. But who cares? We take these things for granted. The only issue is that Baba sits there and says the movie is almost over, and my life is down the drain, because Baba said some stupid thing. Can you see how tiny that is?

CHRIS: So what is the issue behind the curtain for me?

SHARAM: The ego is this imagination in the head that says, "I'm the best. I should get all the attention." You see, I give so much attention to you. Nobody else comes to me and says, "Why do you pay so much attention to Chris?" But if I give attention to someone other than you, like Baba, you think, "I better go and die!"

These are realities. This is the issue hiding behind the curtain. You did not get attention when you were growing up. You hid in the trees, in the woods, and people didn't pay you attention. Your mom didn't pay you attention. Now you want all the attention. It's a very simple thing. Attention deficiency, like ADD. *(Lots of laughter)* It's a simple thing. You don't have any other problems. We found your problem.

"When you don't trust that people can love you, you need to get attention."

—*Sharam*

ONE TINY THING

SHARAM: When we look deep, we see there is only one tiny thing, one tiny issue that is the source of all our other issues, and nothing else. If we see it clearly, there is just one thing. Then, out of that one thing, thousands of other things sprout. *One thing.* All physical and psychological pain comes from this one thing. And this thing is different for each of us. The mind cannot accept, so that one thing becomes very strong when you are in the mind and you suffer. Your whole life is seen through the lens of this issue. When you go out of the mind, when you aren't thinking so heavily, then the acceptance comes. The less you are in the mind, the more is the acceptance, and acceptance is amazing. You feel at home right away, really, really at home. There is nowhere else to go. This is home. Then you really relax. You really let go. You go to ecstasy, and you experience the higher being.

"With the mind you cannot win. You need to breathe energy down to the heart, to the body."

—*Sharam*

JUST A NUDGE

Emotional issues are like slivers in the mind,
One teeny, tiny foreign object,
A speck marring the surface of a soul,
Inciting ridiculous amounts of pain, suffering,
And worrying over.
Kicking
against other's attempts to remove the offender,
With tweezers, needle, and knife
"I can do it myself."

But a master ...?
A master just gives that sliver a little poke here,
And a little prod there,
Allowing it's infectious nature
To grow and expand,
Until,
With barely a nudge,
That splinter pops out of us
Riding a wave of festering thoughts
That's been torturing us for years.

Best feeling in the world.

A BEAUTIFUL MIND?

CHRIS: I go straight to my mind. I can't get rid of my mind. The mind is horrible.

SHARAM: That's only something we learned here. Actually, we didn't say the mind is horrible. The mind is beautiful *if* it is clear. We are working to bring clarity to your mind. Mind is beautiful.

MIND FREAK

SHARAM: When I was hugging you *(Debby),* something just came to me and I'd like to share it with everyone.

When I got up to go, my mind was going a little bit into what I was going to do next and I was excited about preparing something for you guys for Monday's class. When Debby hugged me, all of a sudden that was not important, nothing was important anymore. I was not excited about going anywhere and just became totally here and now. But the mind all of a sudden feels—at that moment when nothing else is important—that it's empty. It can even go to the point of, "Life is empty. There's nothing else. Nothing is worth anything. It's worthless. I want to die. Nothing is good." But remember if you feel like that, that nothing is important, everything is pointless, it's only an indication that you're in the here and now! But the mind misunderstands that emptiness. It thinks nothing is good enough, and I don't want anything, and just nothing excites me. Really, you are here and now in that moment. But the mind thinks of the here and now as nothing.

SHAHED: Death.

SHARAM: Yes, thank you, death.

SHAHED: Here and now is death to the mind and it freaks.

SHARAM: It freaks and it feels that I have nothing here to live for—so just always remember that.

MEDITATION AND THE MASTER

MONA: Which chakra should I work on, and would you please give me an exercise or meditation commitment that works specifically on that chakra?

SHARAM: When you have a strong connection with the master, *any* meditation he gives is the best, because the energy that meditation creates automatically goes to wherever it is needed.

HOW THE PAST KEEPS SHOWING UP
TO SCREW US NOW

CHRIS: I feel left out often and because of this I feel sad and angry at people, like with the incident with Baba. Why is this?

SHARAM: *(To the group)* Very simple logical step. I'm left out as a child. Now, as an adult, it is still a big thing in my subconscious. Then it slips into my conscious mind and I feel left out here. So when Sharam pays attention to Baba, this deep wound comes to the surface, and I hate Baba *(I'm Chris)*. He *(Baba)* talked and made a comment. I didn't like Baba's comment. But this is on the surface. When we open the issue, Chris learns it is not only because Baba made a comment, but because Sharam pays attention to him. She thinks, "It's Baba's time with Sharam now. How about me? I'm left out." Then she feels bad for feeling left out. She thinks it is wrong and makes her a burden to others and decides, "I had better leave, so Sharam can have free access to Baba and I do not interfere."

It always leads to that. She sees her fault, and then she wants to leave. She thinks, "If I hurt people, I better not be here." This is again the same thing. She runs behind a tree. She's that child that runs. It's the circle that goes back to her childhood. "I'm not wanted here. I had better leave."

Now to go deeper with this, somewhere as a child this started because her parents, her mother, were not capable of loving her. That's why I say, if you want to have children, you had better learn love. Now, we need to change that thinking to "My parents were not capable of loving and I was left out under the trees in the cold, because they didn't know how to include me. But I'm not that child anymore. That was forty years ago. This is today. I can love myself. I can see beyond this. I shouldn't run away or blame Baba. I'm either blaming Baba, or if I see it is my fault, I want to run away because I'm no good. If Baba is no good, he better run away. Somebody is no good here." Baba is just Baba. He shares something. I see his excitement about the show and I respond to that. But I still turn around and say hi to Chris. I connect with her because I know how to connect. I am not her mom. I do love her.

A RIGID MIND AND THE THIRD CHAKRA

SHARAM: A rigid mind, which is part of the third chakra, comes from the society and the male part of the family, mainly dad, but sometimes mom is more male. If you are in the heart, you don't have any goals. For example, *you (Kate)* use your rigid mind to create a space, like your sitting, where you can go to your heart and feel free. But if you could be in your heart in the first place, you wouldn't need to worry and plan and bully to create the space for the sitting. You would just enjoy everything.

Also, the third chakra doesn't want to hear anything negative about itself. So it's a catch-22. When you don't want to hear any negatives about yourself, you don't become aware and grow. The only time you can listen and hear is when a little bit of your energy has gone to the fourth chakra, the heart chakra. Then you can grow and open your third chakra more and more.

KATE: How can I work more on my heart, so I come to my heart more?

SHARAM: When you work more, you go to the heart less. The only time you go to your heart is when you let go and have acceptance, not when you work on it. For acceptance, you don't need to work. Meditation and exercises are all excuses, so your mind thinks that it has done something. They really don't make a lot of difference. You just need to accept that everything is ok and be aware of the ego. Also give space to the master to tell you your issues.

"From childhood we are constantly told,
'Don't do this, don't do that.'
The people around us want to improve us.
They want to make us do the 'right' thing.
This makes us feel that we are wrong.
We get wounded because of this.
That is why the human being
is afraid of people criticizing them."

—Sharam

REPEAT AFTER ME: I HAVE A BIG EGO!

In a sitting with Jesse, Sharam told her:

SHARAM: You have a big ego because you expected people to love you, but they didn't, because you didn't love them first. Then you hated them, and that hate was food for your ego, and your ego grew big.

As the sitting continued, he had her repeat what he said twenty times each, in order to reinforce it in her mind.

SHARAM: "Nobody can love me unless I create the love." Repeat!

JESSE: How do you create love?

SHARAM: "I create love by giving space, by loving people and by not being selfish." Repeat!

JESSE: I feel like nobody gives a damn about me.

SHARAM: "Nobody is supposed to give a damn about me. I have to create the love." Repeat!

SHARAM: "This is the glory of the Earth, that nobody can love us unless we create it." Repeat!

JESSE: Why is this the glory of Earth?

SHARAM: Because "I have an ego and by loving others, I put my ego aside." Repeat!

THE EFFORT OF LOVE:
PUT YOUR BACK INTO IT,
THEN LET GO!

SHARAM: Trying to create love works in an indirect way. The effort itself doesn't do anything, but when you try, it doesn't matter to Existence if your love is real or you are just trying. The result is that the person you are loving towards becomes a mirror—they become loving to you in return. You feel their love and you let go, and with let go, love is created. So the effort (or pretending) doesn't create love, but it creates a situation for love to happen.

Love comes with understanding, so if we are not loving, it doesn't mean that we are a bad person. It simply means that we don't understand. We have too much conditioning at work. To understand, we have to be in a state of let go and let go doesn't happen with too much conditioning. So first comes let go, then understanding, and then love.

What is conditioning? It is all the teachings that say you have to work hard and put in a lot of effort. But understanding only happens when the effort drops. That is why going to school doesn't bring understanding, because you have to make a lot of effort and it's all about memorizing. No understanding is needed. You understand something, but only with your mind. That's why you often don't remember it later. When you understand something from a place of let go, you don't remember it either, but it becomes a part of your being. Mathematics or chemistry, they don't become part of your being. They are only part of your memory. Something becomes part of your being only if your understanding increases, and that happens only in a state of let go. From let go, love follows.

"We get to forget.
We get something,
then we forget it to make space
for the next understanding,
the next 'get.'"

—Sharam

DESTRUCTION AND CHAOS

DEBBY: There is a lot of chaos in my life these days, for me and for those around me. Things like cars, stoves, furnaces, and computers are breaking. I don't want to hurt anyone.

SHARAM: When you destroy something for someone—say you are harsh with them, or something happens with them or something breaks and your husband has to fix it—just remember this. If a mystic creates chaos for another, they take a bigger chaos away with the smaller one that they give. So the person could have died, and the mystic just saved them by breaking down the radiator or by saying something a little bit harsh—you save their life. Remember, a mystic always does that. If you are creating chaos for someone else and you are a mystic, you are really helping them. This is the way it's always been. *If* you are a mystic.

What is a mystic? A mystic means someone who has shown over and over and over again—years in and years out—they have shown Existence that sincerely they want to be on its side. It's not the same as someone who doesn't give a hoot about any of this. So remember, a mystic is someone who has come closer and closer to what Existence is. You want to become Existence. You want to put your ego aside. So if you cause a radiator or a car to break, that's perfect. The subtlety of it is we see that it's not chaos, it's perfect.

CONTINUITY FOR THE MIND, CHAOS FOR THE SOUL

Maya was having a sitting with Sharam. The energy was high (positive) and a lot of things were opening up around a specific issue (topic). Then in the middle of it all, somebody called. After the call, Sharam didn't return to what they had been talking about before and the energy was lower or more negative. Maya thought that maybe she had done something wrong and that was why Sharam didn't pick up where he left off.

SHARAM: Society likes continuity on a topic. Existence jumps from one topic to another with no continuity. That's why society in us, which is mind or ego, gets hurt when it encounters Existence. Existence has no continuity on one topic. So Existence, or a master, or a child is happy one second and frowns the next second. But the ego doesn't like this. The ego takes it personally and says either, "It's my fault," or "It's their fault." Basically it's saying, "Something bad has happened and, if something bad has happened, it's somebody's fault." Every time the mind meets Existence, there's a problem for the mind, not for Existence! The mind or ego always says, "Let's do something, so this negativity doesn't happen again." The mind just wants to fix it, but negativity always happens until we become enlightened. Even when we are enlightened, negativity happens, but an enlightened person, knows that negativity is the necessary base for Existence.

EXISTENCE JUMPING

Newborn calves dot pastures
As snow falls through sunlight
Emblazoning last remnants of green
Tipped with reds, yellows, and oranges
Backdropped by snow covered mountains
enveloped in clouds,
Radio announcer:
"Weekend highs are expected to top out in the low eighties."

*"Love means giving space to others
and not always
thinking about ourselves."*

—*Sharam*

GOD AND THE DEVIL

FARIN: Why do you sometimes say negative things to people and then tell them that I am the one who has told you about this negative thing they have said or done, when I never said anything to you about them?

SHARAM: Because I am God *and* I am the Devil at the same time. Devil creates situations. I need to make chaos for you. If I don't make chaos, you will start living and you will forget about growing. *(Sharam has told us over and over again that life is not about living, it is about growing.)*

FARIN: When something negative like this happens, it becomes such a big deal for me. I make it so big in my mind. How can I look at this problem?

SHARAM: When we take things so seriously, they get big. When you take it seriously, your mind starts working around it, so this will be the outcome. We need to give space to people to do, or say, or react to things anyway they will. We need to accept people as they are and know that everything is a play.

FARIN: But I need to be enlightened to be like that, and I'm not.

SHARAM: Ok. Get enlightened. Why don't you? Is it that you don't have the tools to do it *(A master, time, meditation, wisdom classes …)?*

FARIN: *No*, of course I have everything I need.

SHARAM: Yes you do, and all I'm saying is "love." I'm saying give space to others and know everything is a play, an act. Everything.

FARIN: Why should we give space to others? How about others giving space to us?

SHARAM: Because they haven't been given love and space like you have. Anybody who gives space to himself and to others definitely was given opportunities by Existence to be able to do it. Some are given the opportunities, but don't use it. You use it. Many have the potential, but not the opportunity that you have. Also, they have so many blockages they can't give space. If you give space to them, even to their not giving space to you, then you will enjoy. They don't understand, but now you understand. Be playful and know everything is a game. The only lesson here is that Earth is a stage and everybody is playing their own role. If you get attached to your act *(your role)*, you will forget that this is just a game. If someone comes and insults you, or even punches you, if you know this is his script and he needs to act according to his script, you won't get hurt. If you don't see this as an act, you will get hurt and you will hate it. If you understand this, you will understand the master's way of looking at the world. What is enlightenment? Enlightenment means to know that everything is just a play, and everybody is playing their role.

We haven't come here to live, we have come here to go beyond time and living. If you could walk in these people's shoes, if you could live their lives, you would see how miserable they are and how much they suffer. Why? Because they take everything so seriously. If you take life seriously, you will end up being trapped in your mind and your ego, and life will be a struggle, a disaster. Everybody is lonely on earth. Every single person. So don't look to live, because living has failed.

Now as soon as I turn my head, I see every one of you wanting to live. When you are with Master, take it easy. I see people who, even when they are with Master, are so serious, They want to control everything. Come on, give it a break, at least when you are with the master.

We should know whatever is happening is God, everything. If you see this, you won't get hurt.

FARIN: So if we think everything is God, then my anger and hurt are God too.

SHARAM: Yes, even this anger is God, but an unaware God. As a God, you have only one duty here and that is gaining awareness. You can get angry, but do it with awareness. And the only way of getting awareness is by taking things as a joke, a play. Then your anger, too, will be a play. Know that it is just an act. You can get angry, but know that it is just your role. You have one problem and that is taking things seriously. If you don't take things seriously, you will be able to be aware of what you are doing.

IF THE SHOE FITS
AND EVEN IF IT DOESN'T

SHARAM: Any time I put myself in other people's shoes, I love them, and more importantly, I don't get hurt. Also, they will love me a lot too. If I don't put myself in their shoes, I just can't stand them and I get hurt and they hate me too!

FEAR OF JUDGMENT

JESSE: I always have this fear of being judged.

SHARAM: For people to judge you, you usually have to have some negative thing inside. Also, judgment is usually nonverbal, otherwise you would call it an attack or you'd call it criticism. If you are centered, they won't judge. And if they do, usually they will punish themselves in some way. It just won't happen very much. So if they judge you, it's because you have a negative thing inside. When we have a negative thing, we either want to hide it or we show it. Showing it is better because then the master can help you. So judgment is your own thing. You have something negative, but we never, ever, ever want to see ourselves. We just want to look at others. That person judged me. We do have something negative. We know we do. We just don't want to work on that. You just don't care. "They should not judge me." They judge you because they see something negative in you and they think about it. They think about something that they see and if they verbalize it, you don't want to hear it. You don't like it.

ABOUT JUDGMENT

SHARAM: "Write down what you don't like about others, because you definitely have it yourself."

FEAR OF CRITICISM, OF BEING JUDGED

CHRIS: When you suggested that I cook for other people, not just cooking, but that I would be cooking for other people, I panicked and wanted to run out the door. I'm afraid of doing something wrong.

SHARAM: That is very much part of society. We all get conditioned to be afraid of doing something wrong. Understanding goes above that. It really hits our conditionings on the head and breaks them.

CHRIS: My mother, when she got married, moved to a farm in the middle of nowhere. She didn't know how to cook. Her mother-in-law was very critical of her and her cooking. I wonder if the fear my mother had was transferred to me?

SHARAM: Let's look at it. Yes, that has been transferred to you. She had this fear of performing and of criticism before she gave birth to you. That means it was in her soul. Then, she brought a soul that was like her to Earth, and this soul's name is Chris. Your soul was close to identical with that of your mother. You brought the same fears with you. The fear of rejection, the fear of cooking.

Here in the ashram, we break all our fears. We face them and break them. We have to if we want to live happily. If you want to be free, you have to face your fears. That is why you are cooking now. *(To every-one)* I said, "Let's see. Maya, would you help Chris cook?" Maya showed her how and Chris said, "That's easy!" and she did it, and it was fun. With understanding and making things simple, you can have a break-through, you can do it. Then I told you *(Chris),* "If you burn it, great. If it becomes runny, horrible, great!" I told her a story. I had never cooked in my entire life. Then, one day I decided to cook. Somebody gave me a recipe for a dish. I cooked it the first night and it was terrible. The second night, I burned it. I didn't stop for thirty days. Thirty times I cooked, and all the time it was runny and horrible, and the rice was disgusting. I said, "I won't stop." I invested one hundred or two hundred dollars. Every night I cooked it and finally I made it perfect. Then I walked to a place where I knew there was a big ashram. I asked "How many people are here? I want to cook for you tonight." They said, "We are one hundred and fifty people." I said, "I will cook for all of you." I got a lot of onions and potatoes and started chopping. Some of the ashramites came to help. They chopped and I cooked for one hundred and fifty people. I served it myself to them. They loved it and after that, I knew I could cook. We will break this fear of yours. While you are off work for three weeks, every day you will cook. I really would like you to invite everyone to come here and eat with you. Any fear you have, bring it out. This is the place for it. This is the place. *Any* fear. Put it in gear. This is the place where people do not judge you and do not put you down. They really don't. If you think they do, it is you, it is nobody else. So bring out your fears. Let's work on them. The hammer of un-derstanding will shatter all the fear.

*"Healing cannot happen
in the absence of love."*

—*Sharam*

*"Only one person has to be kind
for a situation to change for the better!"*

—*Sharam*

ACTIONS AND REACTIONS

SHARAM: We cannot say that other people have problems. It is *our* actions and *our* behaviors that cause them to react. Their reaction is according to our behavior. If we act with let go and love, their reaction will be friendly and loving too. It is us who causes them to act weird. If we are loving and we have let go, even a crazy or angry person would react very lovingly.

ARDALAN: How about past patterns? Is it possible that people keep past memories and continue acting according to those memories?

SHARAM: No. If you act differently, all the past will be wiped out from their memory. Unless, again, you start doing something that causes them to remember it. Otherwise, as long as you are loving and caring, they will be loving too and everything, even from the past, will change. Always, Existence is fresh unless you are not fresh.

SKIP THE BAND-AID

QUESTION: I feel like my wound has opened in front of people, and I am afraid they are going to hurt me.

SHARAM: The only time people want to mess with your wounds is when you want to hide them. If everything is open and you are not afraid, there is nothing they can do. The only time you get hurt is when *you* want to hide something and someone wants to bring it out and show it to you or others. If you don't hide, they will never mess with you. So no, they are not going to hurt you right now, but if you want to hide it again, they might.

WOUNDS:
THE BENEFITS FAR OUTWEIGH
THE DISADVANTAGES

TOM: Kate brought up an event from a few years ago that involved me. I said that I didn't want to keep reviewing the event and talking about it. Sharam said that I don't want to talk about it because I am still stuck in it; I haven't become complete with it yet. That is why I keep wanting to avoid remembering it.

SHARAM: Both of you have to take responsibility, both of you. You need to know that everything that has happened has, in some way, been to both your advantages. They're win-win situations. If you are hurt by Tom or Tom by you, one part of your lives is not working. One part of your lives is stuck. Just you being hurt is enough, or him being hurt, or both of you. If one person is hurt from the other, both their lives are affected.

Let's say he has some hurt from you, but you have resolved it for yourself. Just the fact the he is carrying this hurt affects both of your lives. You both go through a lot of pain and hardship because of it.

This is why it's so important that both of you become clear and know that everything that has happened is what Existence has wanted, that you see the benefit that has come as a result of this situation for both of you and don't ignore it. That it was worth the situation having happened, because the benefit that was in it for both of you has been much larger than the disadvantages. This is the reality of Existence—whatever has happened in the past has been in both your benefits. Understanding this will lead to your freedom.

This is a general rule of Existence: the benefits of any negative things that happen by far outweigh the disadvantages. The benefits are sky high and the disadvantages are the size of a matchbox. We just stick to the negative and make a mountain out of a molehill, and we become really hurt. Every time you're hurt, something small has been turned into something large. That something may even be something large, but then we make it huge. It was the size of a shoe for example, and we turned it into the size of a swimming pool. It was the size of a swimming pool and we turned into the size of an ocean. This is the truth.

If we see this and understand it, and we go back to the problems that have turned into wounds and look at them together, suddenly you'll see that your lives can really work. A lot of fun things can happen. A lot of expansion can happen, a *lot* of expansion! This hurt that one or the other or the both of you are carrying will no longer impact your lives.

FRAGILE:
HANDLE WITH CARE

ARDALAN: Why do I have so many problems with money?

SHARAM: Everybody gets born into a family according to the needs of their soul. Some people are born into a money-oriented family. Some are born into a culture-oriented family. Some people are born into a money-oriented family, but money is not a problem for them. They have money and money is important, but it is not a problem. You were born into a money-oriented family with problems. You mother has this issue, your father has it, and you were born into this family because you had similar problems as them. At a very young and sensitive age, you got involved with your family's money problems. This has created some memories and some deep wounds for you around money. That's why when I work with you around it, I work in a very subtle and direct way. I work directly but gently with you when it comes to money, because I know this is your deepest wound. When I work around people's deepest wounds, I am always careful and direct. I don't joke about it, and I don't use sarcasm about that wound.

"Higher souls are always there when we accept.
When we don't accept, we refuse them."

—*Sharam*

CALLING ALL MASTERS

ARDALAN: Do all souls on Earth need guidance? Do they need a master, and if so, should everyone be looking for a master?

SHARAM: Yes, every soul that comes to Earth needs guidance, but if you go looking for one, you won't find it. If you feel that you need a master, the master will find you. You don't need to go looking for one.

BEING SPOILED

SHARAM: Being spoiled is a conditioning. We learn to be spoiled and at the same time, we learn that being spoiled is bad. Maybe the only reason people don't like spoiledness is because they are spoiled themselves. The society says being spoiled is bad, but the same people that say it, they are spoiled too. It is very interesting—in fact, being spoiled is not bad. Existence doesn't allow anything bad to happen. What does being spoiled mean? Being spoiled means acting against society or the people around us, and there is nothing wrong with that. Because if a person listens to society or people around them all the time, they become like a machine. By going against others, they start building their self-confidence. This is the first step in creating self-confidence. When your confidence is built, then there is no need for going against anything. As you become aware, you automatically go with whatever is higher, whatever is closer to Existence.

MORE THOUGHTS ON BEING SPOILED

RABIA: What does being spoiled mean?

SHARAM: Being spoiled means having options. When you're rich, you have options. When you are poor you don't have so many. When you have options, you become used to getting your own way. Being spoiled means bullying other people into giving you what you want, either in gross ways or more subtle ways, or any way. Also, when you are spoiled, you are afraid of people wanting to take advantage of you, but really someone who is spoiled takes advantage of everyone because he has options.

THE BEAUTY OF SPOILING

SHARAM: *(To Little Chris)* When you were little, I remember you demanding to your mom that you wanted a certain kind of sandwich at McDonald's, and you were so unhappy when you found out it was too late to get what you wanted. Because your parents always gave you what you wanted when you were small, now that you are older, you don't want as much. Your wants are much less. You have almost passed through this stage of wanting a lot. Everyone has to pass through this stage. Most people do it when they are older or when they get married. But you have almost passed through this stage now and your wants are not as much.

GAMES OF THE EGO
OR HIGH AND MIGHTY

KATE: Last time you told me that a big chunk of my unconscious thinks that I am higher than others. Could you elaborate on that?

SHARAM: When you are around other people, that part of your unconscious becomes active and your heart closes. You feel that everybody is beneath you: God, Master, Existence, everybody. But as soon as you are alone or just with the master, your heart opens and you can breathe. That's why your sittings are very important to you, because that is the only time your ego steps aside and you feel joy and alive.

KATE: Why am I like this and others aren't?

SHARAM: Because you were spoiled growing up, so your ego is bigger and thinks she is higher than others. That's why you can't see your imperfections.

KATE: I understand this, but as you said in my last sitting, knowing and understanding something are not the same as being aware of it. You said that the only way to clean the unconscious is by becoming aware of it.

SHARAM: Yes, understanding is the first step, but the main step is awareness. You understand this, but because you are not aware of how it shows up in your life, that energy is still in you and in whatever you do. You may act as the servant of others or act like a dervish, but because of this energy of feeling higher than others, you want to show that you are the lowest. Nobody can be as low as you. Then, again, you feel you are the best because you are the most humble. So yes, that energy in your unconscious has to change. Not your actions. Your actions are just on the surface. If the depth changes, then the surface will change accordingly. There is one thing you can do: wear the most expensive clothes and show off, but be constantly aware of why you do the things you are doing.

Let's look at something else. You are asking me how not to be like this. You should look deeper and see why you want to change. This also comes from your wanting to be better. Now that you know there is negativity in you, you want to change it. You think, I am this high and mighty person; I cannot have any flaws if everyone is to know that I am higher than them. This is the same game.

KATE: So what happens to working on one's self if we don't want to change?

SHARAM: We want to put the ego aside, not become better. If that's our goal, again we are stuck in the ego. Any goal is egoistic. We should not want any outcomes. Just accept for no reason at all. Become aware of the ego, and accept it. We shouldn't want to stop it or change it. That leads to repression.

Acceptance is the first step. We accept that this is ego, but acceptance doesn't do anything without our being aware of the ego. When we become aware, we become smarter than the ego. If we can do this, the ego will step aside. Meanwhile, you know that while you have the ego, and show off and think you are higher, other egos won't like you. It's just their reaction to your ego.

"Money makes the ego big.
The richer you are, the more ego you have.
Most rich people feel they are better than others.
From a very young age,
they have told us that money and success
are the only important thing,
so we believe it."

—*Sharam*

And, just another reminder,

"The amount of richness you have
is not in the kind of car you drive
or the amount of money you have.
The amount of richness you have
is in how much you are in the moment."

—*Sharam*

"A master does not
tell people to improve themselves.
He only shares his understanding
with the disciple."

—Sharam

ALL OR NOTHING

CHRIS: Things are getting worse and worse. I thought it would get better, but it is not.

SHARAM: You think you get better, but I don't think you get better. We are not here to get better. Either become enlightened or nothing. I'm not here for you to become better. Better is not good enough for me.

SEPARATE YET ONE

CHRIS: I see that nothing has changed.

SHARAM: Nothing has changed. We have made this very clear. Nothing is supposed to change. You will be the same person, but awakened, full of awareness. You will be the same person. One Zen master helped a disciple to become enlightened. The day the disciple became enlightened, he slapped the master and said to the master, "My God, this is enlightenment? It is nothing. Come on. It is just so simple. I am the same person and everything is the same." He got so mad, he slapped the master again. "This is enlightenment? This is all there is? I'm the same." The Master said, "I'm so glad you became enlightened to see that you *are* the same, but you are awakened." Enlightenment is so simple. *(Smiling)* But please, don't slap the master when you become enlightened. *(Lots of laughter)*

Please, it is not about change. Once and forever, I don't want to repeat this. I'm like a broken record, repeating this over and over. It's not about change. You never change. You just become awakened, and the day that it is supposed to happen, it *will* happen.

CHRIS: So I will continue to separate?

SHARAM: Yes. That's why I say Zen is about separation. Forever, for eternity. You will be one with everyone, separated, because that is who you will be forever. Look at the Zen Master . . so separated.

CHRIS: And I will still not feel good enough?

SHARAM: When you are awakened, you feel good all the time. When you become enlightened, you feel good forever. Everything will be so simple. You will be the same person, but you will be totally awake. All the time happy. That happiness comes with awakening, with enlightenment. The day you are supposed to become enlightened, you will become enlightened, happy. No change. Just happy because you are awake. Totally accepting of your separation, of everything. Totally accepting. That's what enlightenment is.

You see, your ego cannot get anywhere. The ego wants to get the upper hand and to complain or prove it knows better, but it can't. The hands of the ego got tied by a simple phrase, "You never change." You will be the same. Total acceptance comes. At that point, you won't even *feel* separated anymore. Enlightenment means oneness, being one with everyone. Separated, but one with everyone because your soul awakens and connects with all the souls, not physically, but soul to soul.

EVEN THE HEART NEEDS
A LITTLE HELP FROM ZEN

CHRIS: How does separating myself help me on my path?

Sharam: Separation is there for the sake of meditation, so you can meditate easier. When you become enlightened, whatever you do is meditation. You hardly ever see me meditate. *This* is my meditation, talking to you. But this is *not* your mediation. Your meditation is when you meditate—until you become enlightened.

CHRIS: I had trouble meditating when you were out of town.

SHARAM: That is a good sign. That means you are connected with me. You want me to be around. The energy that I have helps you to meditate.

(To the group) Chris's energy combined with my energy creates a space for meditation, so meditation can happen. If we were all on the Path of Love here, we couldn't have meditated. That's why when we go to California and stay there for awhile, we don't meditate—because everyone who goes to California is on the path of love. So your being here helps everyone, including yourself.

CHRIS: Do people on the Path of Love need the meditation?

SHARAM: Yes. They see that they need the meditation, because the meditation makes their path stronger. So in any gathering of people on the Path of Love, there must be one Zen disciple too; otherwise their path is weak.

Thanks to you, Chris, you don't know how much I appreciate you. From day one I knew that your being here helps everyone, including yourself. This ashram needs you, and you need this ashram. It is great work. That's how a Zen master comes in. That's your connection with everyone, right there. *(To the group at large)* And that is the connection of her with all you guys. It is incredible how we all need each other. Without you guys, she would be nothing, and without her, you guys are nothing. We can't do it alone. All of us need each other. All of us.

So you are deeply connected. You just have to wake up and see. If your soul wakes up, what I just said, you will see. You will see how each soul here appreciates you, and how you appreciate each soul here. I *want* you to wake up. Enough is enough! There is nothing more important than your soul. There is nothing more important than enlightenment. Everything else we do is on the side, and when you really wake up, you see that everything is so perfectly matched, everything is integrated so amazingly. There is nothing stupid in this world. Everything is perfect. Everything. Every single person, every single thing is so important. The ego wants to say, "I want to be more important than *them*." It is so ungodly. So unexistential. So really, we do have an ashram because of you. We have an ashram because of all of you.

We just have to wake up to it. We have to "wake up and smell the hummus" (Disney's Aladdin).

A CHRISTMAS GIFT

There was a situation at the ashram Christmas party. Farin had set her gift for Sharam against the wall behind him. When she mentioned to him that he had a gift behind him, he didn't pay attention to it. Farin felt he was ignoring it and asked Sharam why that was.

SHARAM: I didn't ignore it. At the time, the gift was not presented to me, you just told me that the gift was over there. Usually, when you give a gift to someone, you hand it to that person. For me, when you told that there was a gift behind me, that gift was just like the other things around me. I didn't ignore it. My reaction was out of freedom. I thought, "Oh good, there is a gift behind me." You see, the curiosity and the excitement people have when they get a gift, I don't have. I don't get excited, because excitement is of the ego.

FARIN: This is so subtle. Because we do have that excitement and curiosity around getting gifts, when you don't have it, then, according to our conditioning, we think that you are ignoring it. But in fact, you are one with it, like other things around you. You are free about it, but we are attached to it.

EMOTIONAL ATTACHMENT
IS BECAUSE OF SELFISHNESS

SHARAM: Emotional attachment is because of selfishness. When you are attached to somebody or something, it's because that person or thing gives something to you. The person or the thing are not that important to us at all, but what they give us is.

As our selfishness becomes less, our attachments become less. So when the heart opens, our selfishness goes away and the result is that attachments disappear. Love is beyond attachment and detachment.

WHO TOOK MY ...?

MONA: Whenever I lose anything, I think somebody took it. What is this?

SHARAM: Even when I lose something, I think somebody took it. It is simple. Someone could be you, too! You move it to another place, and you forget, and you are someone too!

JUST A TINY BIT

SHARAM: It is very important to know that Existence doesn't expect much from us, just as much as we are able plus a tiny bit more. That tiny bit gives us space to grow. Also, all the hardships in the world are just because of that tiny bit more expectation of Existence for us.

*"The meaning of enlightenment is
living here in this world
without any world in the head interfering."*

—*Sharam*

A "MASTER" THIEF

Chris' tape recorder was found by someone who thought it was Sharam's, so they put it in his room. After a few days of looking for it, Chris noticed it in his room and accused him of taking it.

SHARAM: Let me tell you a story. Gurdjieff was accepting new students. A very wealthy woman went to see him. As soon as Gurdjieff saw her, he said, "Give me that big diamond on your necklace." Right away she gave it to him. He said, "Good, you don't have attachment to it. You can have it back." So he accepted her. She had come with a friend. Her friend was waiting outside. She went to call the friend to go in. The friend asked, "What happened?" She said, "Listen, if he wants your expensive jewelry, give it to him right away. He will give it back to you, and he will accept you as a disciple." She went in, and he said, "That is a very expensive thing. Give it to me." She took it off and gave it to him. He said "Get out of here. I'm not giving you your necklace. I don't want you as a student." He never gave her necklace back.

CHRIS: I am afraid of punishment because of what I said to you. Why would I say such things?

SHARAM: It comes from unawareness. It comes from the world out there that is inside of people. The poison. You see, it is not about the tape recorder being important, because it is not for you. The voices of out there are important. If Sharam took my tape recorder, he is a thief.

CHRIS: I should be getting more aware, not less aware.

SHARAM: You are not becoming less aware. As a matter of fact, you have the courage to say things now. Before, you were so afraid. The courage comes from more awareness. Now you share what you feel, so we can work with it. That is advancement. Being more courageous to share, and then having the willingness to go and listen to the tapes of your sittings over and over again is awareness. You really are dedicated to working on yourself. These are really positive things. If I had ego, I would not like those things you said to me, but I am declaring it as good. It was a positive thing. I'm telling you that you have more courage. It is really good. I am really happy. There is no punishment, unless you punish yourself. Isn't it funny that you think I will punish you, whereas we create our own world totally?

We really create our own world. You have created your world. Everything. There is not one world; there are millions and millions of worlds, according to how many people there are on Earth. One person sees and hears one thing, while at the same time, you are seeing and hearing something entirely different. That's why there are so many problems, so many clashes. But a master lives in the here and now. The meaning of enlightenment is living here in this world without any world in the head interfering. So you create everything about you. If I punish you, you create that too. Why do you create it? Because you feel guilty. When it happened, I addressed it. I went right into the guilt, because I knew the moment you did it, you felt bad and at some level you would punish yourself or you would try to force me into punishing you. Nobody punishes you. You create the world.

CHRIS: I don't even think I was aware of how bad my behavior was until you told me.

SHARAM: Yes, the subconscious was aware of it. The reason I told you was because I knew your subconscious would disturb you. I am telling you that it doesn't reduce my being a master if you say that I am a thief. Then I am a thief master, a master that is a thief. Believe me Chris, I am only working with your ego. I am not interested in your tape recorder. I addressed it, and it is over.

"Incorrect and yet,
no mistakes at the same time."

—Sharam

DON'T TRY TO DO THE RIGHT THING

CHRIS: You said the other day that my ego is big. It *is* big. You said it is supposed to be and that I am supposed to make it bigger. How do I let it get bigger without doing horrible stuff like accusing you of being a thief? The ego is ugly and the bigger it gets, the worse the stuff that is coming out.

SHARAM: By knowing that there are a lot of things that you don't understand. So you do something, like this situation, and then we talk about it; I explain it to you, and now you have a new understanding. Don't try to do the right thing or become obsessed with what you *should* do. Do what you are going to do, and then we talk about it. Just don't take it personally when I say something to you about your ego. Do not defend yourself. Good questions are good. When you say, "How do I not do that?" that is very good, but when you defend yourself, that is where you go wrong. When you fall apart and feel guilty and then you are afraid of punishment, that is where you go wrong, because the fear will take all your energy away.

EXISTENCE TALKING

FARIN: I cannot express myself. I'm so afraid of expressing.

SHARAM: You know how I express myself? I trust. I trust Existence. That's why I'm not afraid of expressing.

FARIN: I don't know what the result of my expressing will be. If I say something, it might raise hell.

SHARAM: I don't know the outcome either, but I just trust Existence; I know Existence is in charge, so I know whatever happens, Existence wants it. Even if chaos happens, it is good.

"You can worry,
or you can let Existence worry for you."

—*Sharam*

"Knowledge is memory.
Learning comes from experience.
Learning is hard."

—*Sharam*

ALL ABOARD!

SHARAM: We go on missing life, because by the time we decide, the train has already left. Life is momentary, and each moment needs its own decision. If you wait, the moment is gone. We have been taught about the ultimate values. We have not been taught about the immediate, about responding to the present with our total hearts. And never be afraid of committing errors. If a person really wants to live, he has to be ready to commit many mistakes. They are natural. Nobody comes with a ready-made mind. The mind grows through situations, through challenges. The hesitant mind never grows, it remains retarded.

But we have been taught not to commit mistakes. We have become so afraid of committing mistakes, that we hesitate. Never be afraid of committing mistakes and hesitation will disappear. In fact, one should be willing to commit as many mistakes as possible. You will learn through them. Otherwise, how is one going to learn? Learning is through trial and error. There is no ready-made knowledge which can be given to anybody. And don't waste time thinking how to drop this hesitancy, simply drop it. From this moment start making decisions. Many will be wrong, but that is how one grows.

Sometimes one goes astray, and that is perfect. For example, if Adam had not gone astray, there would have been no world. Feel thankful that Adam and Eve went astray, otherwise there would have been no Christ. There would have been no Buddha. Original sin is not a sin at all, it is a way to grow. So never waste time in too much thinking. Each moment needs your response. Respond. Then whatsoever happens, is good. Respond with whatever you have right now. Your understanding, your maturity—just respond with whatever you have. Be ready to commit as many mistakes as possible. They are just fantastic.

See, your problem is that you are afraid of making mistakes. That's why you sit there and keep worrying. Committing mistakes is perfect. Then there is no worrying. All worrying is because we have been taught that committing mistakes is wrong, and here we are again at the one hundred and eighty degree rule saying commit as many mistakes as you can. When you really make this a part of your being, you won't worry about anything. All worrying comes from fear of committing mistakes. And that is the greatest mistake, to not commit mistakes.

SHAHED: You know when you make a mistake and there is another person involved, I always feel this rush to fix it. "Oh god, I made a mistake and I have to fix it." This can haunt you for a long time. How do you deal with that?

SHARAM: This is another teaching of society, that other people should not get hurt, or you should not make a mistake on someone else's account. These are all wrong teachings. If you make a mistake and something goes wrong with someone else, they needed that mistake to learn and that is really good. It's not you that's running the show; Existence is running the show. So why would you get upset?

SHAHED: I guess it's the ego wanting to look good, wanting to be able to say, "Hey, I'm really not as bad as I looked right there."

SHARAM: Yes, exactly. Because if everything and everyone is Existence, and everything is run by Existence, and you are Existence, and someone gets hurt, they needed that. Existence wanted them to go there. You were just the one who helped them to get there. There are so many people and everyone has to help everyone else. If you make a mistake and it hurts another, they will grow from that, and you will grow from it too. It's all about growth.

HAVING FAITH OR HAVING FEAR

SHARAM: Having faith means trust. It means being sure. The only thing that causes our trust to become weak is fear. When we have fear, we are not sure. Then we cannot trust the situation. So either there is fear or there is being sure. There is nothing else but these two. If you are sure of something, then you trust and you have faith. If we are sure that everything is right, then everything will be right, but if you have fear, and you are not sure, then everything will be wishy-washy.

Existence is a reflection of us. For example, if you are a person who worries about money, then all of a sudden you will become a person who owes lots of money. And the way that you start owing people is weird. Somehow the circumstances in your life will cause situations where you suddenly you owe money to people. I have experienced this. At a time when I was worried about not having enough money, my landlord would come up with every little excuse to charge me more money. No matter how much I paid him, he would come up with new ways that I owed him. One day I told myself, "Enough is enough, I need to stop worrying." Then everything changed. That was the turning point.

Fear creates exactly the situation that we are worried about, because Existence is a mirror. So, every situation we are in is a reflection of us. It reflects us, so we can see ourselves and come to know ourselves. That is the goal of life really, to know ourselves. But everybody ignores Existence. They break their mirrors. Instead of looking at themselves, they blame others; or they create something to be entertained or distracted by, like watching TV, reading a book or a newspaper, going to the movies, and so on. Some of these entertainments they call a virtue, like reading a book. Others are a sin, like watching a porn movie. In doing so, they create more conflicts inside, distracting themselves even more, again keeping themselves from looking in that mirror.

WINDY DAYS AND DANDELION PUFFS

A thought, a dandelion puff,
Harmless, but for wind,
Spreading seeds
In a thousand and one directions.

HIGHER LAW VERSUS LOWER LAW

SHARAM: There are two sets of laws: Earthly laws and higher laws. We can only practice one of them. They cannot be practiced together. Earthly law says, for example, that if you have this amount of money and you spend half of it, you won't have enough. If you spend all of it, definitely you will be miserable. As long as we think like this, we won't let the higher forces or the higher law come into play.

What is the higher law? Higher law says, if you have let go and you are open, you can give easily and receive easily. So higher law says, if you spend this amount of money and you don't worry about it, it will come back to you a thousand-fold. But to have the higher law work, we have to leave the lower law behind. They cannot work together. They are contradictory. Wanting to have both of them together only brings chaos. It won't work.

Even when you look at them logically, you can see that they won't work together. Lower law says, if you spend money, you won't have it. Higher law says, if you spend, you will be given a thousand times more. In the lower force, if you spend your money, you won't have it, and if you don't spend it, you will definitely have it. And this is true. The amount of your money won't change, it won't go anywhere, but it won't increase either. It will always be the same amount that you had. If we want to have more money, we need to be free about it. But remember, wanting to be free and being free are not the same thing. Wanting to be free doesn't mean being free. Again there is an attachment to wanting to be free.

We need to know that we create our world; it is not anybody else's fault. It is ours. If there are problems in anything we do, it is because we have created those problems. If I am struggling with money right now, I have created it. If I have emotional problems, I have created it. But we usually think this is the master's fault or someone else's fault. Any person who thinks that is a crippled person.

GETTING STUCK IN OUR HABITS

DEBBY: I'm getting stuck. An example: the lilacs are blooming. I love the smell of lilacs but lilacs die. I don't want the lilacs to leave. I love the smell so much. I actually feel upset when they go. The same thing has happened to me with the school board cutting the music program at Chris' *(Little Chris)* high school. I'm so upset about it.

SHARAM: You get upset when the lilacs leave because when they were there, you felt that you didn't connect with them deeper. You have this idea that, "Wow, I should really enjoy these while they're here," and then, because you didn't, you hate for them to leave. You think, "Why didn't I use that time really being with these flowers?"

Because if you really could spend deep moments with them, when they leave you, will be happy. It's the same with the band. If you really were not busy, or thinking of other things, if you really, really were with the band, when it leaves, you will be happy. It will be fine. You think that there's something else that you need to get from the band that you didn't get. I wish it would stay longer so that I would just get that thing that I missed.

DEBBY: I'm hearing what you're saying, but I'm not getting it. I don't feel that.

SHARAM: You think that if the lilacs stay longer that's better, or if the music program continues, Chris will be happier and that will make you happier—that it's not about the fact that you missed it, it's about the fact that you want it to be there all the time. Right?

DEBBY: Yes, that is true. I want it to be there all the time. This I see.

SHARAM: So this thing that you want to be there all the time is because you couldn't be totally with it in the first place. But you don't see that and that's fine. The mind doesn't go there. The mind thinks, "Well, my son is happier, so you should keep that." But Existence gives us *exactly* what we need for our soul every moment and it takes away those things that are not useful anymore. People get used to something and they take it for granted or things become a habit. That's why Existence takes them away, so that we will see something deeper and become more aware—so that we will realize they were becoming a habit or that we were taking them for granted. But then we fall apart.

DOING BUSINESS AND
BEING MEDITATIVE AT THE SAME TIME

ARDALAN: I want to expand my work, but it requires me to think all the time to come up with new ideas. How can I do this thinking all the time while being meditative and in a state of let go at the same time? It seems there is a contradiction here. How can these two meet?

SHARAM: You need to make your work like your meditation. Your work should become your meditation, which means that you should bring your totality to it while, at the same time, having let go in whatever you do.

ARDALAN: My problem is that I think my job is against my path, that it pulls me away from my path. I think that business and making money go against spirituality, so it causes me to have a contradiction, a fight inside.

SHARAM: You need to know that if you bring your totality to whatever you are doing, you will go beyond the mind. And going beyond the mind is everything.

ARDALAN: It seems so far from me. Have you ever seen me go beyond the mind?

SHARAM: Yes, I have. Every time I come to your store, you go beyond the mind.

ARDALAN: In that case, I need you to come to the store all the time *(laughter).* What should I do other times?

SHARAM: If you are able to go beyond your mind when I am there, then you have the ability to do it on your own. If you couldn't go beyond your mind, it wouldn't happen even when I was there. So there *are* times that you have become total in your work and have gone beyond your mind. You just don't know it. In those moments, you don't realize it, because you are already beyond your mind, and recognizing that you are beyond the mind requires the mind!

COMMITMENT

ARDALAN: I think everybody has to have commitment to their job or to whatever they are doing. If we don't have commitment to our work, we won't be able to have commitment to our path either.

SHARAM: When we talk about commitment, there is a higher aspect that we need to understand. Let's say, you are doing your job but something happens and you need to close your store and attend to that thing. If you do it happily, then Existence will take care of everything, because you show to Existence that you have a higher commitment. We have only one commitment and that is to Existence. This commitment causes trust. If we trust Existence, everything will be fine.

Remember, when we talk about Existence, it includes everything and everybody, not just the master. We usually accept things and awkward situations from our master, but not from anybody else. We need to know that Existence includes everyone, our master and other people too. Existence uses egos and non-egos for our growth. Even when someone makes a very hard situation for us and is doing it totally on purpose, even if they have a plan to destroy us, even *that* is great and needs to be accepted. That person is Existence. We cannot say that our master is Existence and because of this, we accept situations from him, while at the same time claiming that other people are not, and therefore we cannot accept the situations that they have created. Everyone is the helper of the Existence. No one is separated from it. Everyone is one with it.

WHO IS THAT WOMAN
IN THE WINDOW?

SHARAM: One thing, very interesting, is that when you grow, before you get to know who you are in any one moment, you have already passed that level. You have grown to a higher place. Your mind can't catch up. So basically, you don't know who you are. People who don't grow, know exactly who they are. They hate cream cheese, they like bread, they are a Republican, they are this but not that, *but you constantly change.*

The mind always wants to grab onto, "Well, I am this or I am that," but you can't because you keep growing. This can create a chaos. We always want to know who we are, but we can't because we are growing. Every minute, every day, you are a different person, all of you. So we have to forget about knowing who we are, or even thinking I shouldn't be doing this or that. Every day, Existence is showing up in a different way for you.

SHAHED: One way this happens for me is in talking to people. I was talking with my brother the other day about nothing important, but I was so uncomfortable just trying to talk to him. It was just a normal everyday conversation, but it was torturous trying to come up with something meaningful to say. When I am with people, I find it hard to just settle down and "be" with them.

SHARAM: Is that because of the expectation that you've got to be meaningful? Because most of the time, talking with people isn't meaningful.

SHAHED: Maybe. I want to feel present with them and I don't.

SHARAM: Because you have that expectation. Presence simply means not having any expectations. Just know that ninety-five percent of the time, talk does not become meaningful. If it does, that is rare. Most people prefer to chit chat. It makes them feel good and they like to hear what you have to say.

SHAHED: Well, usually I just ask questions about them because I don't feel like I am doing much, just meditation and family stuff, and I can't sum up the work we do here in a short time. I don't even think I could talk about it very well, even if I had all day. I feel inadequate and want something interesting to say.

SHARAM: Ok, again, with the inner work, always there is something new, and you have forgotten what happened yesterday anyway. So you don't know what to say because the old thing (*understandings or what you did yesterday*) is gone and the new hasn't come yet. There is just the moment, here with this person.

SHAHED: It feels like, if you are present in the moment, every moment would be meaningful, but it's not for me. Maybe I don't know what meaningful is.

SHARAM: The mind has to let you free. The mind has grabbed you with this idea that you *should* be doing this or doing that (*something other than what you are doing*). You are doing a lot of things. It's not like you are sitting around doing nothing all day. If you were, you would be enlightened.

There are these lines of conditioning that say, "I have to have something to say like everyone else. 'I'm making lots of money,' is that meaningful? That's rubbish. We are conditioned that we have to have something produced to tell people. This is only a conditioning.

You, Shahed, do something in the moment and then you forget it. You are advancing your soul, cleansing your soul, and the soul is talking to you, but you can't hear it. The moment you hear it, you hear it, and it is none of the other people's business anyway.

Interactions are shallow. Most people are not ready to go deep into connection. They want the shallow. Very few people want the depth, and if you try to go there with them, they feel uncomfortable.

DON'T WORRY AND
WHATEVER YOU SAY WILL BE GOOD
OR, MIND: THE ULTIMATE EVALUATOR

FARIN: Why, after class or a group meditation, when you ask me how it was for me, when I answer you, it seems so weak and superficial? When I talk, I don't like it. I think everybody's talking is wonderful, but when I talk, I weaken the space. Why is that?

SHARAM: When you start talking, your mind starts evaluating what you say as you say it. While you are talking, your mind is evaluating constantly. You wonder if what you are saying is good or bad, or you think, why did I say that? Your mind is constantly at work evaluating what you just said. Not only that, but you bring your mind in at a time when it is difficult to bring it in, right after meditation. So when you talk, you don't like it because of this mind, but when I listen, I like it so much. If you aren't worried about it, whatever you say is good. It is just that evaluation that makes you think it is weak. Evaluation is like an exam. At the end of every semester, you have an exam and you get evaluated. It brings lots of tension and worry. That is what your mind is doing.

SPEAK UP, THEN LET IT GO

SHARAM: If you are sure that a person is wrong about something, anything, and that they will create problems for themselves or others, if they keep going the way they are going, tell them what you feel. That is totally your love. If they don't listen, and they go against what you have said, then Existence wants them to fall into that ditch. So they go and fall into the ditch and get their lesson from it. If you are kind and loving, you tell them what you feel and leave them to make their own decision. So you say something, and they insist on what they said, and you let it go.

This is a good policy to follow. These things will come up more and more. So share things one time, but remember that the other person is entitled to go and fall in that ditch.

REFLECTIONS OF THE MIND:
THE IMPORTANCE OF EXPRESSING YOURSELF
TO STAYING IN THE MOMENT

Leila, who has been married before, is having problems with her current husband.

SHARAM: We gather a collection of hardships and negative things in our memory cells.

Then, when something happens, our mind, instead of reflecting what actually happened, reflects according to those negative memories. Our concepts of what is happening are not the reality or the truth. It is just those negative thoughts. For example, we will reflect experiences of an ex-husband onto a new man who is acting a little bit harsh now. When our mind is like this, just reflecting the past, we start having problems with others; we can't see them as they are. In this case, we can't see the new man for who he is.

But these are just the mind's reflections. If you had been strong from the very beginning of your first marriage, if you would have been able to express yourself freely in the moment instead of just bearing with things, then you would have become a very strong woman who would have kicked her first husband out. You would be so strong, everyone else would be counting on you. A person who does not have the power to express themself and is not strong, thinks that it is everybody else's responsibility to make things good. This person thinks that she can't do it. She is just ready to like or hate someone based on their actions, because what they do determines if she can be happy or not.

For example, you used to be afraid of fights. You avoided any problems, but now you are getting stronger. Now you are living with people and there are struggles, ups and downs. In working through these ups and downs, you are becoming stronger. You are not the Leila from the past. That Leila was a mouse. You are not a mouse anymore. All these struggles and ups and downs are helping you.

THE IMPORTANCE OF BEING BALANCED

LEILA: Why do we have so much respect for a strong woman?

SHARAM: Because a woman is female, and when she becomes strong, it means she has become balanced. When anyone is balanced, we love and respect them. But if she becomes too strong, then her male side will be stronger than her female and again she is unbalanced. Then again you won't like her.

STRENGTH AND SOFTNESS

DEBBY: I'm feeling uncomfortable opening up right now. All the attention is making me uncomfortable.

SHARAM: I'm so glad that you opened up. The whole purpose of us being here is about opening up and understanding deeper, so I'm glad that you are opening up. Maybe we think that it's a sign of weakness to open up, but it's not. It's a sign of strength. When you opened up just now, it showed strength. Society has said when you open up, when you cry or when you say something negative, it's weakness. But it's totally the opposite.

DEBBY: I feel like I'm letting everybody down because I can't be centered.

SHARAM: Right now you are not letting everybody down. You are letting people up. You are lifting people's hearts.

DEBBY: I'm seeing, sitting here, that no one here or at home judges me at all.

SHARAM: You know why people accept you? Because you are strong and you are soft at the same time. If you were only strong, they would be afraid of you. They really would be your enemy, but they would act like your friend. But if you have softness *and* strength, people love you and respect you at the same time. Yes, people love you.

(To everyone) We can sit with our jealousy, with our competing, with our comparing. We can feel bad and we can stay with these feelings for eternity, and never change, or want to do something for ourselves. Really. When you really want to do something for yourself, you won't feel bad, you won't hide anything. You'll express it: "Hey I'm jealous," but you'll share with a sense that you want to get help from it. You humble yourself. Then Existence will help you in the most beautiful, refined ways. You don't need to sit with your negativities and hide them, or boil in them, or get angry, or just hate someone and not share it. Come forth and do something for yourself. Really. You can't do it with anger. You won't get anything from Existence. You can't do it with feeling sorry for yourself. You can't do it with fight. You *can* do it if you really want some help. Existence will help you immensely. Don't fall apart. Come forth, express your feelings, be honest. Don't be afraid of other people's judgment. That is their own problem and believe me, those who judge in one way or another will punish themselves. You don't need to worry about them at all. I really want this group to do something for themselves. My connection with all of you has changed. You will soon see that.

SHARAM: *(To Debby)* There is a strength with the softness in you that makes you really trust me and trust Existence, and because of this you are gradually trusting yourself more. When you trust yourself fully, you will trust the whole world and deep trust is enlightenment. Thanks for the strength and softness that have created this trust. I just love you very much Debby, very much.

"The only reason the negativity feels bad,
is that we associate negativity
to be something undesirable.
We don't want it. It is bad.
I think negativity is great.
I love it. It's a chance to grow.
So when negativity comes, wow!"

—Sharam

CLIMBING THE LADDER OF NEGATIVITY

CHRIS: Everyone else here seems so positive. Why do you say it is a good thing, when I am negative?

SHARAM: How do you think they can stay positive? Because you hold down the fort on the negativity. Somebody has to do it. Without that, how can we be positive? The negative has to be in one pole for the positive to happen. They are in positivity now and you are keeping the negativity. Now we are all going to transform you to positivity. We will all meet in positivity. The negativity is not necessary any more. That is why you came forth—to change it. It was necessary until a minute ago. When you are in negativity, it is needed; when you come out of it, it is no longer needed. Then we go to a higher level. At this higher level, very soon you will become negative again. Then because of that negativity, other people go to positivity and then you come to a new level, a higher level of positivity. It goes on and on and on *(standing on his chair and pointing higher and higher)*. This is how it is. This is how we grow. It is beautiful. No complaints.

CHRIS: But this negativity feels really bad.

SHARAM: The only reason the negativity feels bad is that we associate negativity to be something undesirable. We don't want it. It is bad. Some people think negativity is great, like myself. I love it. It's a chance to grow. So when negativity comes, wow!

CHRIS: You have compared me to some people who are very negative. I don't like their negativity, and I have heard you talk about their negativity as if it were a bad thing. If I am like them, how is my negativity ok and theirs is not?

SHARAM: Because you are sitting here working with it and they are not. If you work with negativity, negativity becomes a blessing. If you don't work with it, it becomes terrible. If they were here, wanting to work with it, it would be great. Anything that you want to work with is a blessing. If you don't want to work with it, it becomes a burden.

THE FOUR STAGES OF NEGATIVITY

SHARAM: There are four steps in negativity.

The first step is when you are totally in negativity. You can't see anything beyond that, just total negativity. The second step is when you are *not* totally in negativity, but you project a lot of negativity into different things. You constantly bring negativity to situations. I'll give you an example. You plan a wedding and there are lots of wonderful things. People are enjoying themselves, having fun. The food is incredible; the best foods you could ever want are at the table. You can eat anything you want. The tables are beautiful. Then you go to grab a drink and you see one hair on the table where they serve the drinks. *One* hair and you start making the whole night out to be horrible: "This is disgusting. Why aren't these people considerate? This is a mess. This wedding is terrible." This is not *totally* negative, but you bring negativity into anything you see that is not up to your standards. Then we have someone who is normal. When you see something negative, you mention it, and then you pass it. It is ok. Let me give you an example. I bought a brand-new car, a cheap car, not very expensive. I drove it out of the factory and the same day I picked up my friend, an old man eighty-five years old. I picked him up, and while we were driving I put my foot on the brake. It squeaked. The brake made lots of noise. My brand new car. So

I told my friend, "You see? The brake is already making noise." And he asked, "Does the windshield make noise? Does the wheel make noise? Do the tires make noise? Does the seat make noise?" I said, "No, everything else is perfect." He asked, "So what if just the brake makes noise? Look at everything else that works perfectly." After that, I totally let go of anything that was negative. That is the fourth step and the fourth step is incredible. Whatever is negative, the person will not pay attention to it, would not even look at it. After that day, in the car, I never cared about the negative. I saw how stupid it is. When you get this, life becomes so great. You enjoy life. The fourth step is the best.

FALLING ASLEEP DURING MEDITATION

CHRIS: The other day I was meditating, and I kept falling asleep. I started condemning myself for not being able to stay awake and watch my thoughts.

SHARAM: When you sit and fall asleep, you consider that a negative thing. I don't. I consider that a very advanced thing.

CHRIS: You have said that thought continues in your sleep, in your dreams, but I'm not conscious of my dreams. I don't remember them. So I am not witnessing in my sleep either.

SHARAM: It's because you are very judgmental about sleep. Unconsciously you are really judging the sleep. The only reason you are not witnessing your thoughts, which are dreams when you are asleep, is because you consider it bad. Existence wants you to sleep, so you can witness your thoughts when you are asleep. This is very advanced, but if you think sleeping is bad, witnessing can't happen, because you keep judging it. Sleeping is great. When you are dreaming, even the dreams have to be witnessed, so I'm saying to you, if you fall asleep when you are meditating, that is a great opportunity to witness your dreams.

CHRIS: So how do I change my subconscious?

SHARAM: By simply watching that judgment when you are falling asleep. Just tell yourself it is fine. It is great. There is nothing wrong with this. There is a reason for it. This is how you change the subconscious—by telling yourself consciously that it is ok.

Try it. It will take maybe three weeks if you try it every day. Fall asleep and watch. Tell yourself, "Sleep is good. I am going to witness my dreams." After three weeks, if you do it every day, you will see the result in remembering your dreams or you might not see a result. You come and share with me and we will go from there.

I'M CHEAP! WHAT TO DO?

RABIA: I'm cheap. What to do?

SHARAM: Cheapness and overspending or being irresponsible with money are two sides of the same coin. So, what to do? First you have to accept the facts about yourself without getting emotional, without crying or condemning yourself. If you can do that you have taken the first step towards going beyond these two.

The next step is understanding. The more we understand, by and by the more the mind changes, and then the inner changes accordingly. So what is the understanding here? When we are cheap, on the surface or from the point of view of the mind, it means we don't trust Existence. At a deeper level, which is the soul, something else is going on which is all about love. What is going on is that deep inside we know that if we expand our spending, our ego will take over. It will say, "Look at me, I'm so generous, I'm such a hot shot." We think that being a big spender means being a great person. But if we spend too much, we are being irresponsible. By being cheap, we prevent that, but neither one of these poles is ideal.

THIS MESSAGE IS BROUGHT TO YOU BY GOD

SHARAM: Existence keeps giving us messages. If you don't want to hear what Existence is telling you, you go to your emotional body. You become emotional. If you want to hear it, you pay attention to see what the message is. Anyone can do anything around me, and I can get the message of Existence in their action.

CONDEMN THEM ANYWAY

SHARAM: If you don't want to condemn someone, you should condemn them and not worry about it! That acceptance will lead to no condemnation anymore. We get stuck in condemning. And even now, if you condemn so you won't condemn anymore, still you are stuck in not wanting to condemn, and it won't work. Condemn joyously and let it go.

THE WEAKEST LINK

DEBBY: This week my back is really hurting. It's been a difficult week—many things are going badly and I am dropping deeper into "This is bad." My mind just won't stop. My back is hurting more and more.

SHARAM: You are noticing that when you are negative, your back hurts.

DEBBY: Yes.

SHARAM: When we believe something is bad, and it gets more and more bad, it makes us very worried. So worried. You see, if you were an evil person, when something is bad, you would enjoy it. Oh good! (claps his hands together) Let's make all this bad happen. But remember, we are on the path because we believe in goodness.

But because we've been taught to be good, something that we believe to be bad sucks a huge amount of energy out of us because of the anxiety that comes with it. We think, "This is horrible," and we worry so much that we use up all our energy. Then less energy is available to the body, and your weakest point falls apart. Your back is your weakest point and it doesn't get the energy it regularly gets.

It is so good that we have a weakness. This is our barometer, this is our yard stick to remind us, "Hey, you are using too much energy." In fact, that's why the body has been given to us, to have a weakness. So when the energy goes into too much worrying, that weak point starts hurting to tell us, "Hey, you're worrying too much." Every person has some weak place in the body and that is a blessing. Otherwise, we'd worry ourselves to death. If nowhere hurt, we'd worry, worry, worry and then one day, we're dead. There would be no limit.

That pain, that weak point, in your case the back, is a lifesaver. So thanks God. It keeps you healthy and is helping you towards enlightenment. We should treasure our weak point in the body.

DEBBY: Thank you. Thank you so much. I feel more relaxed now with this understanding.

"We resist Existence. We resist what is happening
in the moment and then the soul suffers.
This suffering spills over into the body
in the form of karma,
and the body gets hurt by this karma.
It gets damaged and diseased."

—Sharam

"Working on yourself means getting more energy.
When you understand something
there is all of sudden an opening,
a clearing of karma or blockages in the soul.
With this clearing,
lots of energy climbs up the chakras
and healing happens,
both physically and emotionally.
If you take a break from working on yourself,
so your body can heal,
really healing cannot happen.
Livia is healing her hip,
but while she is healing,
she gets angry and upset too.
If she doesn't work on herself to
break the blockages this anger creates,
really she's damaging herself more."

—Sharam

THE MECHANICS OF UNDERSTANDING

SHARAM: When you understand something about yourself, when the light bulb turns on and you "get" it; or when you feel connection with someone; or you hear a song or think of a memory that makes you happy; etc., your vital energy climbs up the main artery of your soul. This happens because the two sides of your brain, the male and the female, connect. As the energy climbs it breaks some of the karmic blockages on the way up which means healing. Also, when the energy reaches the heart center, which is the source of real happiness, you feel good.

APPRECIATION:
THE ULTIMATE VACUUM SWEEPER

SHARAM: I just want to talk about appreciation. Appreciation opens a huge space in the unconscious for all the karma inside to come to the surface and leave. And the opposite, demanding, does totally the reverse thing. It vacuums karma from outside and brings it inside. *(Lots of laughter)*

FINALLY, A CURE FOR ACNE!

LITTLE CHRIS: I was wondering about my acne, what causes it, and if there were any breathing exercises to help with it. I'd really like to understand it more deeply, why it's there.

SHARAM: Skin problems come because the mind is worried. So when we worry about this and that, that worry eventually shows on our skin or face. Skin is the most outer part of our body so the worrying hits the skin first thing. Just because of worrying. But you look so relaxed right now. Maybe at school or at home you worry about something?

LITTLE CHRIS: It definitely has something to do with school, because when we have holidays it starts to clear up. I think it's just because I don't like to go to school. Is there an exercise I could do to help fix it, because it really does bug me a lot?

SHARAM: Yes, if you could stop worrying gradually this will go away. Then of course when you take deep slow breaths, the body relaxes more, and the skin gets better. So do seven deep full breaths, three or four times throughout the day. Then all of a sudden the body feels so relaxed and the skin gradually follows suit. It won't happen right away.

It takes twenty days of three or four times per day. Then you will see that gradually the skin gets better.

LITTLE CHRIS: How come some of my friends stress out and worry all the time and they have no acne and I worry a lot less and have some?

SHARAM: Some people's stresses hit much deeper. For them, worrying may affect the kidneys or the liver or heart, and for them it won't show up until much later, when they are older. And when it shows up, it just kills. The acne doesn't kill, it just shows, but it will soon go away. So having acne is a great thing. If you are a person who can express yourself—you can talk, you can express, you are outgoing—then it comes to the skin. If you are more inward and you can't express yourself, then those things go deep. The disease inside doesn't show up until you're forty or fifty or maybe even sixty. Then something fails and they have to operate and get it out.

Chris, you look so different.

LITTLE CHRIS: I get that a lot.

SHARAM: You have become much more gentle. You are gentleman now. That's what mysticism is really about, how to become more gentle—a gentle woman, a gentle man.

DEBBY: Chris, do you see yourself as gentle?

LITTLE CHRIS: Sometimes.

SHARAM: Anyone who is gentle, sometimes they have to be tough also. Gurdjieff was a really tough man, but really gentle too, amazingly gentle. You can't have only one side. If you are always gentle, then you are not real. It's not real. On Earth, you have to have both. I love you very much Chris.

LIVING FROM THE CENTER

QUESTION: Is it true that when you work with a master, you don't have to worry about bad things happening to you?

SHARAM: A master is between the disciple and Existence. The only way that a master protects the disciple from Existence is by opening the subtleties with the disciple. It is not that the master opens a big umbrella to protect the disciple, or has a big hand to cover the disciple from harshness. Master opens issues and brings the subtlety out. When you understand, you go to your center and, in the center, the problem gets resolved. In the center that karma gets cleansed. Bad things happen to remind us of our issues. If you resolve an issue, you don't need a reminder. If you don't resolve it, you do.

RESISTANCE IS A CHOICE

CHRIS: I know I shouldn't resist, but I *do* resist, all the time. How do you go beyond that resistance?

SHARAM: Resistance, believe it or not, used to be a choice. It has become unconscious, but still it is an unconscious choice. You unconsciously choose to resist. You could simply not resist, but somehow in the past, resistance paid off. That is why we keep resisting. When we resisted then, we got what we wanted. It only takes once. Once. You wanted an egg, or you wanted a chocolate. Mother didn't give it to you and you resisted and fought. "I want a chocolate. I really want a chocolate. Please, please, give me a chocolate." Then Mommy gave you a chocolate. Now as a child, every time you can't get something you want, it comes to your mind: "Oh, resisting. That will pay." Even if it doesn't pay off for many times, because it paid off once you will try it anyway. What else is there to do? It might work. Then, if you resist many, many times, it works again. Mother gets fed up and says, "Have this." If it works twice, it's a done deal. You have learned resistance. Then you start resisting more and more, just out of habit. It becomes less and less conscious and more a knee jerk reaction. When resistance becomes unconscious, it doesn't pay off anymore. It just makes us suffer more and more and more, and we don't even realize that we are doing it or why.

There are no techniques in the world that can help with resistance except awareness. When we bring awareness, we do not resist. Resistance shows a lack of awareness. There are two ways to awareness. One way to awareness is that you can simply bring awareness in at any moment. If you are resisting, notice it. Anger is a good sign of resistance. If you find yourself angry, stop, ask yourself, "What is going on here? Oh, I'm resisting right now, hmm." Just that awareness is enough. Or, if you are resisting a change of plans or which movie to go see, notice it. Any little resistance will do.

Another way to awareness is that you meditate and wait for the awareness to come in the future. We can bring awareness into any moment if we want to, but we have to choose to bring it.

WORLD CLASS RESISTER

RABIA: I am a world-class resister, what to do?

SHARAM: So, you are accepting your resistance?

RABIA: I want to be able to do that, yes.

SHARAM: Ok, if we want to stop resisting, we can't. But you can accept that you are resisting. You can do that. We can't stop our resisting because just the desire to stop resisting is resistance in itself. You are resisting your resistance. When you accept your resistance, you simply say, "Yeah, I resist and there's nothing wrong with it."

RABIA: But there *is* something wrong with it because it puts a wall between us.

SHARAM: But if you accept that you are resisting, your energy goes towards accepting. You see, you are resisting all the time. You don't always see it. Normally, you're just walking along and you're happy and everything is great and fine and you're laughing. But even then, there is resistance, otherwise you would be enlightened. You resist all the time, because you think. The mind is always on, and the mind means resistance. You are not aware of your resistance, but if for any reason you become aware of it and you consciously accept it, a beautiful thing happens. Not only do you cut your resistance that you are aware of in this moment, but you also cut the root of the resistance that you are completely unaware of. Then, all of a sudden, you are not resisting at all. You are not thinking and there is every possibility that you will become enlightened.

So it's good to resist and then accept this resistance. It benefits you double.

A few days later, Rabia read this sitting out loud in class for those who hadn't heard it. Sharam made these comments.

SHARAM: Let's make it more simple. For example, let's say that right now, you really, really, really hate Livia, or you really don't like this thing. You are resisting Livia. She did this horrible thing. "I hate her." I don't promote this though: Livia is nice and kind,*(Lots of laughter).* So what to do? Go to your room, close the door, close your eyes and sit there. Sit straight, don't bend your back, and just be available to any feeling or thought that comes up. Whatever happens in the moment, be available to it. As you keep watching your resistance, all of a sudden this energy of resistance gets released and combines with the energy of attention and goes deep within you, releasing both your anger at Livia and the resistance that you do all of the time and are not aware of. These two energies become a great force in you and all of a sudden you're not resisting at all.

SHAHED: So you said that we say to ourselves, "I'm available to look at this," and then what happens?

SHARAM: A miracle happens and you feel good.

SHAHED: So you don't necessarily have to understand why you hate Livia or why you're mad at someone.

SHARAM: No, no, no—don't analyze, just go into the feeling that you have. Don't analyze, because that brings your mind in, and the mind takes a lot of energy. We need the energy to do the miracle.

LIFE AFTER DEATH AND REINCARNATION

LIVIA: You have said in the past that when we die, the mind (ego) dies with the body and the soul enters a state of bliss. If this is so, why does anyone choose to be reborn into a body?

SHARAM: When we die, we are unconscious. We cannot think after death. Destiny carries us. We die unconscious, so "nature" brings us back to the body to give us another chance at consciousness. If we become "supernatural," "super conscious," then we can choose after death whether to come back or not. We have the choice to become conscious *while we are living.* Only in the body do we have the option to become conscious.

REINCARNATION
AND THE POPULATION EXPLOSION

TELLY: About the whole reincarnation thing—if all souls are just re-cycling themselves, what about the growing population of the Earth? What's going on?

SHARAM: Every piece of sand is alive. We just don't see that there is consciousness there; it is very dim. This sand has to evolve and become a plant, a fish, a rooster and then finally it becomes a human being. So every single piece of sand is working towards becoming a human being. But human beings need to go to the higher states. It's only af-ter reaching enlightenment, becoming free, that a soul doesn't need to return to Earth. But most humans don't reach enlightenment, so they have to come back. The old souls who have been human beings for many lifetimes die, they don't become enlightened and they have to come back again and again. Also an enlightened soul can choose to come back as a human being. So the population keeps growing because every single piece of sand is becoming one person—becoming a hu-man being. And that's why there are so many people.

SELF-CONSCIOUSNESS:
THE OPPOSITE OF SELF-CONFIDENCE

SHAHED: What is the root of being self-conscious? You know, in a negative way—worried about things in relation to myself with others.

SHARAM: The root of it is unconsciousness, not being conscious. Self-conscious means you are conscious of yourself in relation to others. Worrying is being self-conscious. For example, you project a disease, "Oh, I know I have this disease." This is self-conscious. Every time you project something onto yourself you are then self-conscious. So self-consciousness is a kind of disease.

One has to not put their identification on the body, on the mind, on the emotions. When you identify yourself constantly with your body, you are self-conscious. If you are afraid of death, you are self-conscious. If you hear something and then you become emotional, you take it personal, that is self-consciousness too. So it is broader, bigger than what we normally think.

SHAHED: I was thinking of the self-conscious of—let's say you look at me and then all of a sudden, I am self-conscious in an uncomfortable way.

SHARAM: That's the normal way that people use it. You become conscious of yourself, but you don't have self-confidence, so you feel something is wrong with you. Why are they looking at me? It comes from a lack of confidence. I remember the Fonz. He goes to comb his hair and he says, "Ehhhhhhh. Perfect!" *(Laughter)* He has self-confidence. So self-consciousness means not having confidence in ourselves.

Self-consciousness is the opposite of self-confidence.

SHAHED: I'm just wondering if it has its roots in perfectionism or what? I felt it last night when you asked us to spend some time connecting with one another. It came in and out. Fear of approaching others.

SHARAM: How does perfectionism relate with being self-conscious? You think that if you approach someone, there is always that fear that they might not want it or you shouldn't. You become self-conscious. Maybe they don't want to be touched or maybe I'm suffocating them.

When you don't have self-confidence, you will be self-conscious, and perfectionism comes in when you want everything to be perfect.

SHAHED: Even perfectionism would come from a lack of confidence too wouldn't it?

SHARAM: Yes, perfectionism is the desire that everyone wants to be the most perfect, the most beautiful, gorgeous. Your body should not smell. You have to have all these things so people will like you, and if people like you, then you feel like you are perfect. When we are a child, we are bombarded with all the ways we are not perfect. "Listen, you did wrong. Naughty, naughty. This was not good. You're no good. What did you do that for?" All of that is a memory in the head reminding us that we are not perfect. In many things you do, then, you will become self-conscious. Maybe this is wrong. You have lost your self-confidence. These are the voices of the past, and perfectionism comes from that too. You were criticized for so many things and now, as an adult, you want all those things to go away. You don't want to be criticized.

It also comes from wanting to become God. Wanting to be perfect. The most perfect on Earth. In a sense it is going to help people. It brings them to the path and gives them a desire to understand. Perfectionism is good, but at one point we have to let it go because to be perfect is not possible. God is not perfect. If you want to be God then you cannot be perfect.

"The wisdom of insecurity is that
it makes us more aware.
We are more aware because
we are afraid of rejection."

—*Sharam*

ONE THOUSAND AND ONE
GAMES OF THE MIND

SHAHED: Why is the desire to compare such a big thing in us?

SHARAM: Comparison basically means mind. Mind compares. We should make a sign here of all the stuff that the mind does. It would be very interesting. The mind does hundreds of things. The biggest things mind does are judgment and comparison. The reason? Mind just does them. If you come out of the mind for any reason, if you go to the heart, then you don't do any of these things. If you dance or jump up and down, or feel connected with me and come to the heart, then all these thousand things that mind does fade away. That's when we say someone is egoistic or not. Being egoistic means these one thousand things of the mind are happening. That's what we mean by big ego. Anything that gets you out of the mind, like meditating, connecting with me. *(To Chris)* Like right now, your heart opens and opens because of understanding. Understanding gets you to the heart, and the mind lets go of you. Kisses help too.

EXISTENCE USES EVERY OPPORTUNITY TO SQUASH THE EGO

CHRIS: Why do I have so much fear?

SHARAM: Comparison. Fear comes from comparison. Not always. Fear comes from other things, too, but one of the very strong ways fear comes is through comparison. You compare yourself in the classroom with someone who gets A's and are afraid if you don't get an A. There is fear of failure, of not being good enough. Someone else might become first in the class and you won't. There is fear.

CHRIS: I am afraid of being jealous. I'm afraid of all those negative feelings.

SHARAM: Comparison brings jealousy in with it. With comparison, we think we are worse than others. Why does comparison come in? If you are dancing like everyone else, you don't compare. If you are not doing what they are doing, you compare, and then what happens? "I'm not good enough. If I am not good enough, I fall apart." When we compare and feel we are not good enough, we close ourselves. Then, every happiness from outside will not enter. Watch your comparison. Every time it does the same ugly thing. I'm so glad you are seeing that comparison is so very painful.

Different people have different issues. Frank doesn't compare. He just puts people down. When I see his face go into that place *(Sharam imitates the facial expression Frank is making)*, then I have to draw him out from that place, that place of putting people down in his head. He will not fall into the emotional body because he is a man, so it is easier to draw him out of it. He constantly judges people. Comparison is much gentler, but it hurts *you*. Judging others hurts other people more. It hurts him too, but not as much as comparison.

CHRIS: But by comparing isn't your energy also hurting the other person?

SHARAM: If you feel jealous, then the jealousy would hurt them. On the surface it hurts them, so that they can look at themselves. So it has wisdom. Everything has wisdom. So in the long run it has a benefit. In the short run it hurts others, so they get to look at themselves. Existence doesn't waste! Nothing goes to waste. Everything gets used for a higher purpose. If we look at this very shortsightedly or linearly, it is hurting them. If we look at it broadly, circularly, then we see that everything gets proper use. Basically, then, we shouldn't worry about other people. We should look at ourselves. If we hurt other people, it is good for them. If we *don't* hurt other people, it is good for them. Whatever happens, we just trust Existence. We just look at ourselves and work with ourselves.

WASTE NOT!

Got a new composter yesterday
Two hundred dollars on sale,
Very sheik and efficient
Two weeks tops from counter to useable compost,
Selected a spot just outside my kitchen window
Up on a little hill
And set it up,

How responsible I feel,
Nurturing the environment
And my garden,
How self-sustaining and green.

Now, at my kitchen sink,
I gaze excitedly at
Each thin strip of carrot,
Leaping from my peeler,
Landing squarely into today's Starbucks' cup,
Both soon to be soil in my garden.

Looking again out my window
I notice a movement
A bear. How cute …
"Honey, come quick, a bear!"
… lumbering and sniffing …
headed … Oh no!
Straight to my composter!

Shoving my newly arrived,
And very resistant husband
Towards the door,
I cry, "Quick, stop him!"
"He's going to kill the composter."

Giving up on getting my husband
Through the door frame,
I rush back to the window
Just in time to see
That bear rear up on his hind legs
And squash my composter flat,
All the air just whooshes right out of my lungs.
"He's eating all of yesterday's
Seven percent composted scraps," I rasp.

Then,
Satisfied that all the tasty morsels are gone
He squats
Leaving me a large steaming package
That just screams,
"Two weeks!? Ha! I can do it in a day!"
Before lumbering off to the neighbors.

ANGER AND RESPONSIBILITY

CHRIS: I didn't feel angry when you were in LA, but when it got closer to you coming back, I felt angry again. Why?

SHARAM: Anger means you put your responsibility on others. When you take full responsibility, you don't get angry. When Master is around, you put your responsibility on him. When he is not around, you take the full responsibility.

THE INS AND OUTS
OF ANGER AND DEPRESSION

CHRIS: I still have this cycle where I get really angry and then I go into depression. Yesterday, I was so angry. Then I fell into depression. Nothing mattered. I didn't want to do anything. I didn't care about anything. I still feel a lot of anger this morning.

SHARAM: Anytime we get angry and we don't understand why and we don't shout and yell at the person that we are angry at, the next thing that happens is the anger subsides. Then this big ball of energy falls deeper in you and causes a lot of commotion in depth. We call that depression. Remember, anger is energy on the surface coming out. If for any reason, it doesn't come out, it gets repressed and becomes depression.

I'M ANGRY!

SHAHED: I am really angry. I have been watching these last few weeks, all these feelings of not being good enough, all this inadequacy, all this doubt, and constantly not feeling good enough. Then, out of this not feeling good enough I compare, and then I hate those I compare myself to because I don't feel good enough. I'm angry, but I'm I blaming them.

Ok, then we have said here that when you are angry, you are releasing karma, but that if you are blaming, you are creating karma. Also, working on the book, I've had this quote in front of me for four weeks now that talks about how anger means not having acceptance for anything, So, I'm just wondering about this anger thing.

SHARAM: Ok, when the karma is leaving, you don't need to accept anything. The karma is leaving. But every time after anger, right after anger, acceptance comes. If you watch, you will see. Every single time after anger comes, acceptance follows. During the anger, no acceptance is necessary because the karma is leaving. If you accept before anger, the karma doesn't leave. So not accepting during anger is wonderful. Without anger, karma will just pile up, and we don't want that.

When you accept, what happens? You don't create karma, but the existing karma doesn't leave either. That is the job of anger, to get rid of the existing junk. So when you are angry, you can't accept, because if you do, then that stuff cannot leave. There is a time for acceptance and a time for anger.

Always, after a period of intense, or even not so intense anger, acceptance comes. It is amazing that when you go to anger, Existence balances it with acceptance right away. How much acceptance depends on how un-accepting, how angry, you were before. A lot of anger: a lot of acceptance. They balance.

SHAHED: Ok, so as I was sitting there angry, instead of yelling I sat with it. I just allowed it, and it turned from that hot, "I want to slap someone anger," to this really cold, cold anger. It made me feel really powerful. I wish I could feel that power and be ok with it, but instead I go back to this "I'm inadequate" thing and I start to feel guilty for being angry. I'm not aware of the acceptance part. I only feel guilt.

SHARAM: That guilt comes from acceptance. It is very interesting. Because you accept, then you think, "Why did I do that?" That, in a sense, is acceptance. That is putting the ego aside. If you didn't put the ego aside, you'd want to kill everyone. That's what the ego loves, to destroy others. Feeling guilt comes from surrendering.

So there is acceptance, surrendering, and then guilt. You don't see the accepting. You don't see the surrendering. You just see the guilt, but the other two always come first. First the ego has to step aside and you accept, then the mind kicks in and says it was wrong, and you feel guilt.

A RIPE FRUIT

SHAHED: I keep watching that inadequacy, the lack of self-confidence. When am I gonna stop feeling so inadequate?

SHARAM: You are making the ego stronger. Inadequacy means that you see the fact that you need to make it stronger. It needs to go deeper. It means that you are looking at this fact and you want to do something about it. You need to make your ego stronger. You need to make it more ripe. Self-confidence (ego confidence) makes the ego ripe, and when it is ripe it is like a fruit—when it is ripe it falls by itself or you just give the tree a little shake and it falls.

So you are making your ego ripe. That is a big step. If the ego steps aside, that's huge. This is where you are. You are really looking at the ego. Ripeness doesn't mean bigger.

SHAHED: … it goes from more of this maniac thing to this stand up tall kind of thing.

SHARAM: Have you noticed that people who have a lot of self-confidence really chill out; they kind of let go, because their ego is stepping aside. Self-confidence, very powerful self-confidence, will lead to no-ego. Without self-confidence, we really struggle. People who have self-confidence just accept. Everything is fine. We call them cool, but not a fake cool.

SHAHED: Can I achieve this with this little person inside who is so jealous and hateful?

SHARAM: Yes. This morning I was talking about being a mouse. A mouse is someone who is always hiding everything. Inside they are dirty, but they are scared to share. Courage means to be able to express yourself, not hiding from anyone. With you everything is on the surface. This is courage. This will ripen the ego.

EGO AND TRUST

FARIN: In the past I didn't have self-confidence, and any time I wanted to go to new places and meet new people it was a big deal for me. I used to feel weak with no self-confidence, but during my last trip it happened that I met new people, and these people were kind of high level people in society. Before, I would have been concerned about it, but this time I noticed that I had more centeredness and inner strength. I was not feeling weak or lower. I was not feeling higher either. I was feeling that I am in a right place, and this place is what Sharam has created for me. I noticed that lack of self-confidence happens because we are not satisfied with who we are.

SHARAM: This is so subtle to feel strong and not egoistic at the same time. When we don't trust Existence, it is egoistic. What does it mean to not trust Existence? When we control things, we are not trusting Existence. Or when we feel lower or weaker, or even stronger and higher, this is ego too. Existence does not have higher or lower.

*"Fear of rejection is really the fear of
not being number one
which is the most important thing
on Earth for the ego."*

—*Sharam*

FEAR OF REJECTION

CHRIS: I noticed in the exercise we did the other morning *(having an inner dialogue with those I have issues with)* how much my fear of rejection completely rules me. Lately it shows up as being afraid to go back to Rabia's room for fear she will reject me.

SHARAM: Yes, fear of rejection is definitely deep. Ego has some original laws and some by-laws. This is an original law. This is one of the first few things involved with the ego. Ego wants to be number one. "I am the best of the best, the highest of the highest, king of the kings. If somebody doesn't see that—if I go to that room and they don't acknowledge me as number one—I fall apart." If somebody wants to suggest that you are not number one, you go to either fight or flight. Because you are afraid of fighting, you tend more toward flight. "I feel like I should just leave."

If you feel adequate and strong, then you don't need to be number one. If you feel one with Existence, then nothing matters. If the ego is feeling weak, it wants to save face. It creates a fake strength. It pretends. First, the ego gives you the feeling that you are not good enough. "I am afraid to go back to Rabia's room for fear she rejects me." It is always telling you that you are not good enough. Then it says, "I am going to fight for you. I am going to pretend and act like I am very strong and important. I'm gonna give Rabia hell if she rejects me." But what it is really telling you in a subtle way is that you are not important. The ego is harming you from two sides. It is a double edged sword.

CHRIS: Is that why you said the only time I can go back to her room without fear is when I put my ego aside?

SHARAM: Yes. When the ego is not there, then there is nothing to worry about, because you don't want to be number one. If the ego steps aside, permanently or temporarily, then who cares about being number one? You are free of the fear of rejection. If someone says something negative about you, when there is no ego, you hear it, you talk about it, you open it. But when there is ego, you get upset. "How dare they not see that I am the best? I am much better than them."

If you truly believe in a master, that means somebody who has put their ego aside, and you truly trust them, then, with the master, you don't think that you are number one anymore. So you are not afraid of rejection from the master. You have given the master space to be higher than you. You are afraid of rejection from people that you think are below you, but if truly somebody is higher than you, you are not afraid of rejection anymore. This is why everyone is afraid of rejection, because they think they are better than others. "No way will I give them the opportunity to put me down."

CHRIS: You said that I need to learn to give love without expecting it back. That seems tied into this, because that means I'm not afraid that others will reject me. Whatever they do is fine. Am I at the stage where I can do that?

SHARAM: It doesn't matter if you are at that stage or not. If I were you, I would just do that. Then if they reject you, you are going to see how your ego is involved. It is an opportunity. You are always at that stage, because whether you can stay centered or not doesn't matter. You want to watch and see what happens to you . It is exciting to find out where you are.

CHRIS: And, if I respond negatively, it is all just my ego? It has nothing to do with them?

SHARAM: Yes. You want to be number one and they don't let you, so you respond negatively, with anger or running away or some other reaction. It is all about being number one. Buddha would say desiring. *(He laughs)* Good old Buddha.

REWARDS OF THE EGO

Just wanted you to know
I'm better than you
You may have a cold,
but I have the flu.

REJECTION:
AN OPPORTUNITY TO GROW!

CHRIS: I wonder why I still have so much fear of rejection.

SHARAM: Fear comes only because you think of rejection as bad. If you get rejected you hate it, but rejection is as good as getting accepted. We have been taught that rejection is bad, so we can't imagine that it is good. Rejection is good. If we think of it as good, it won't hurt us. It will makes us happy. We are just really sensitive and have been taught that if you are rejected you are no good, you are horrible. We take it personally right away. There is nothing personal. If it is personal, people will tell you. If they say you are horrible or terrible, then we can do something about it. If we really want to work on ourselves, we won't be afraid of being rejected. If we don't want to work on ourselves, if we just want to be and not grow, then there is a big fear of rejection.

People who really want to work on themselves are not afraid of rejection. They consider it as a stepping stone, an opportunity for understanding themselves deeper. In doing so, they show Existence that they are here to really grow, not here to just be. I'm really inviting you to look at life differently, from the standpoint of growth and excitement. Growth means excitement.

WISDOM

SHARAM: Wisdom means understanding the subtleties of Existence. You are wise when you understand the wisdom, the reason behind everything that happens. You become in tune with Existence, you understand it. It's brings light into the darkness.

A CIRCLE AND A DOT

CHRIS: I don't seem to be centered at all this morning. It seems like it takes very little for me to drop to a lower place, right now.

SHARAM: That means it takes very little for you to work on yourself. If you stay centered, because the ego is there, the ego picks up the center and destroys it. You are better off dropping now and going to a higher center. So if it takes very little for you to drop, you really need that. Existence is guiding us. Your soul knows exactly when you need it. It is perfect. If it doesn't happen for someone else, that means they don't need it anymore. We just have to trust Existence. What I do is bring trust to you by bringing understanding to the situation. So, you drop. You go to negativity. What happens? It means that right now there is a blockage you need to pass. If you understand that, when you drop, you'll love it, you'll enjoy it. When you bring acceptance through understanding, you become happy, even when you are down. It is magic. It is a miracle. This was a tangent, the bigger picture. Let's go back to your case. You drop, when you need it.

CHRIS: I seem to be dropping a lot right now.

SHARAM: You need a jump. You have come to a small blockage, a cluster of karma. You want to go up, but you can't. You keep hitting the blockage. If you drop a little further, you get momentum to break these blockages and tiny karmas leave. They will leave whether you accept the fall or not, but acceptance makes it faster.

CHRIS: What are these karmas from?

SHARAM: They could be from anything. Recently you were unhappy. Something happened so you were withdrawn.

CHRIS: When we have cleaning day here at the Ashram, I always feel excluded.

SHARAM: When we have this feeling of exclusion, then we have a problem. We bring this problem and make it other people's problem. It becomes very selfish. We push it on people. Here, we are all connected. We are all one family, but you think you are separated. You can be angry or upset, pull away, go to your own corner, go to work, go outside, but you have to learn here that if you do that stuff, other people get hurt too. You hurt people. It's as if one link in the chain is broken, the rest of the chain becomes loose. This is how you push your issue on to them. You feel excluded and then do something to make others feel bad.

CHRIS: Do you want me to just change my actions?

SHARAM: Observation. Observe them. If you observe them, you don't change them. They change by themselves. Remember, guys, if you observe something, automatically, automatically, automatically, automatically, it changes everything into a win/win situation.

CHRIS: You said you have to be centered to observe. How can you be centered when you are in the midst of your issue?

SHARAM: You can't be centered, but also you can. If you really want to, you can. Remember, our souls have inexhaustible energy. If we put this energy into anything we want to happen, it will happen. Right now you don't want it to happen.

CHRIS: How do you change your ego so you want to?

SHARAM: For that, there is no technique. Just make a decision and do it. That is the best technique. If you want to, you can do it. Write down "I really want to do it. I want to make a decision to observe my feeling excluded."

CHRIS: I have been in a mode lately where I feel I can't do anything.

SHARAM: Just because you don't want to. You become female in front of this, become helpless, you become little. It is like the little boy who was peeing in his pants all the time. The doctor asked, "Why are you peeing?" The kid said, "There is a huge monster that comes to me. It is so big I am afraid. That's why I pee." The doctor asked, "Would you draw the monster?" He drew a big, big circle. The doctor asked, "Where are you?" He put a small dot next to the circle. Johnny said, "This is me and that is the monster. That's why I pee." The doctor said "Now, let's do something. Draw yourself very big and write, 'This is me, Johnny.' Put a small dot and say it is the monster. Do this twenty times. 'Me. The monster. Me. The monster. Me. The monster.'" Johnny did this. Then Johnny didn't pee anymore because the monster became so little and he became so big. You are in front of this huge thing, this task, and you become very little. "I can't do it. It is too big." Let's reverse it. Make yourself very big and the task very small. You can get a piece of paper and pen. First you make the task look very big, and yourself very small. "I can't do it." What's the task? To remember that when you feel excluded, you become upset. Because you are upset, you can't be centered to look at the exclusion. So 'being upset' is big and the little dot here is Chris. When this is so big and I am so little, I can't do anything about it. Now we want to reverse it. Use two pieces of paper where being upset is big and Chris is little. Now we reverse it. Chris is big and being upset is little. You do this twenty times. After twenty pages, you get the feeling you are bigger than being upset. So when you are upset, it is nothing, just a tiny dot. You are bigger. You become centered. Then, with the centeredness, you look at your main issue, which is feeling excluded. If you observe it, it will transform. You need to stay centered and observe it.

BEING IN TUNE WITH EACH OTHER

ARDALAN: I have a problem with working with Farin. She is not in tune with me. I don't know why she is like that. When I am around, she is not in tune with me. She makes mistakes that when I'm not there, she doesn't make.

SHARAM: Let me tell you something. The human ego is very interesting. It does funny things. The ego is not in tune with anybody. When someone is told that they need to study and get a degree, they don't want to do it. Even if they do it, they have to fight with themselves to get it. It takes a very big effort and a very hard fight to get it. If you say to someone you should become a doctor, he becomes a nurse. If you say to someone you should become God, he becomes a doctor. So humans' egos automatically want to do the opposite of what they've been told. I say, "Get enlightened," but everybody is resisting it. Ego doesn't want to listen to anybody.

Now when you ask Farin to do something, she doesn't want to do it. This is so unconscious. She doesn't even know it herself. She thinks that she is trying to do it, but in fact she doesn't want to do it. This gets worse when a man and woman are in relationship. As soon as you have sex with someone, you will never be in tune with that person. Because as soon as two people have sex, their ego wants to dominate the other. If you want not to be in tune with someone, go and have sex with them! It's the best way to avoid being in tune. You are in relationship with each other, so you won't be in tune with each other. You know that if you have a good temper (if you didn't have a temper) it is good, but you don't do anything about it. She knows that if she learns everything about the store, it is good, but she doesn't want to do it. And we cannot tell anyone to not have ego. But by looking at these things and opening and understanding them more, little by little we are cutting ego's head with cotton (gently.) Because the ego has run the show for a long time, we need to be so subtle to take the show out of his hand. We need to be more advanced than ego.

THE NATURE OF EGO: FIGHT!

SHARAM: When you are hurt, it means that your ego is up. Ego comes up first, and then you get hurt. Only ego gets hurt. If the ego doesn't come up, you don't get hurt. And remember, all egos want to fight with others. If there is no fight, the ego thinks he or she is dying, so the ego always needs to fight, to have an enemy. If there is no enemy outside, then you *(the ego)* will create one in your dreams and thoughts. If not there, you will target "evil" in general as your enemy. Wives and husbands fight with each other because they are closer to each other, so they let their guards down more. It is easier for them to attack each other.

We are here to release ourselves from ego, not to be in the hands of ego.

APPRECIATION

SHARAM: When we connect with people, it's wonderful. But, grad-ually things go bad because over time, we stop appreciating what we have with these people. And because we don't appreciate, we lose that powerful connection, the nice thing we had. If we start appreciating, we will bring all those good things that are gone back! So this is a gift of Existence, to take back great stuff when we don't appreciate it, so we can learn the lesson of appreciation, or—we can live a low—quality life.

ARE YOU READY?

Chris had been invited into a private meditation with Sharam and a few others.

SHARAM: This is a big step for Chris and an important lesson for everyone. If we are demanding or we ask, "Why can they do something and I can't," Existence knows that we are not ready yet. But if we are happy with what we have, Existence gives us a lot more of everything.

APPRECIATION

SHARAM: People learning about our weaknesses and using them against us is just a way of Existence telling us we are ready to grow one step deeper and to understand more. But we are afraid of it. That shows we are not ready to grow. Almost everybody is like that. When we understand that this is the love of Existence, then we *are* ready to grow.

*"When we bring the ego in,
we are inviting others
to bring their egos in as well."*

—*Sharam*

THE INS AND OUTS OF HATE

SHARAM: The ego wants to criticize us or someone else all the time. But in reality, there is nothing to hate: Existence does everything. You simply go to the pocket of hate inside your emotional body, and you feel hate. You hate everyone and you think everyone hates you, but the reality is that nobody hates you. Here everybody loves you. Everyone. If you think somebody doesn't like you, you are bringing your ego in and then they don't like you, because you brought your ego in and nobody likes ego. It is all up to us. It is nobody else. Nobody else is ever doing anything to us, ever.

THE EGO IS CRAZY

CHRIS: The ego is crazy and yet, even though we are here to look at ourselves, we still fight looking at ourselves like crazy.

SHARAM: You are right. Ego is crazy. The craziest, craziest, craziest. It is so crazy. I was just reading that many people read magazines about movie stars that have a scar or this or that problem. People love to read that. Why? Because the ego knows that these people are hot stuff, and if they are a mess, then I am better. The ego just loves it. Dirty things about important people, everybody will read. Magazines make so much money from that just because the ego likes to put down those who seem higher than us. The ego *is* crazy. It is always watching out for itself. It always wants its own benefit. Always. Always. Always. Don't you think it is such a crazy thing that you always want your own benefit, you always watch for yourself. That is so crazy. This is separating yourself from God. Separation.

FINE LINES:
EGO OR PASSIVITY

SHARAM: There is a fine line between passivity and putting the ego aside. They are almost like each other. Stream puts her ego aside with Debby and me, that's why she feels good to be with us. But she also withdraws sometimes. That is her ego withdrawing and inwardly hurting her. This is what we call passivity. Every time the ego gets hurt, we either attack or withdraw; and inwardly the ego starts fighting us. When we are more female, we withdraw; this is passivity. When we are more male, we attack; this is aggression. Both ways hurt us and others. In general, ego wants to hurt one way or the other!

FIRST AND THIRD CHAKRA

SHARAM: The anger of the first chakra only arises when one is in danger. Anger for the person in the third chakra is when they don't get what they want. People move between the chakras depending on the situations they find themselves in. We say that the third chakra is better because it is close to the heart. This person can go to the heart and the lower chakras. Someone in the second chakra can get to the first chakra and maybe the third, but getting to the heart is more difficult for them. Being able to move between more chakras is inner vastness—you have access to more places in your soul.

MR. SANDMAN LEND ME SOME SNOOZE

LITTLE CHRIS: I haven't slept hardly at all the past few nights, and then I'm exhausted when I have to go to school in the morning. This sometimes goes on and on. What's happening?

SHARAM: Does this happen often?

LITTLE CHRIS: No, only sometimes. Sometimes I can use some of the breathing exercises you've taught me, and they help me fall asleep.

SHARAM: Good. We travel from different chakras depending on what has happened to us that day. When you are in the first chakra and you do the exercises, so much fatigue goes out of you that your body doesn't want to fall asleep. For example, Livia's siblings, they are both in the first chakra. We are doing these exercises, and they just can't fall asleep. They have a hard time because they are cleansing the first chakra.

If you cleanse the second chakra, you fall asleep like a baby. The first chakra is male so when you cleanse it, you have so much energy you want to be awake. When the second chakra or the fourth chakra cleanses, you just fall asleep. The female cleanses and you just relax. But when you are in the first and third chakras and you are doing some cleansing, you are wide awake. The male becomes strong and of course cannot rest.

_____
I AM NOT THIS BODY
_____

SHARAM: If we separate ourselves from the body and the mind, all suffering will go away. Go inside and say to yourself:

> *"I am not the body.*
>
> *This body is not me."*
>
> *Picture the body falling far away, far away.*
>
> *It is going farther away, even more distant.*
>
> *You are standing somewhere and the body is moving down and farther away.*
>
> *The body is going down more and more and more.*
>
> *Going down, away.*

With this simple exercise, suffering can be transformed. An inner change will occur that leads you to the Beyond or happiness. Suffering will separate from you.

ONE EASY STEP

If you want to be ecstatic
I recommend a change of tactic
I don't mean to be didactic
(I had to look that one up too)
Just want your life to be galactic

The change need not be drastic
Not magic
Like pulling a rabbit out of a hat trick
Doesn't require the aid of a hypnotic
And will definitely reduce expenditures on chiropractic.

It's ease may baffle the analytic
And wake up the anesthetic
And whether atheistic or agnostic
When you realize you feel fantastic
You can't help but become acrobatic

I hope you won't become apoplectic
Or find the answer anti-climactic
I tell you what,
I'll accompany it with some acoustic
Well here goes
Ahem
Just become an accept … tic. :-)

HAPPINESS,
DON'T LEAVE HOME WITHOUT IT!

SHARAM: Acceptance is the way to come to the moment—the only way. Acceptance happens in two ways, with effort and naturally. Either you try to accept, or it is intuitive. Intuitive means that you have accepted so much that it comes naturally to you. This form of acceptance is much stronger. If you have to accept with effort, the effects are not as strong as when it just happens. But acceptance with effort is still valuable because it is the first step to transforming to intuitive acceptance.

With understanding, deep breathing, or reminding yourself that everything that happens is for a higher reason, you bring awareness to the moment. This helps the mind to step aside and leads to acceptance.

Thinking is a subtle form of resisting and resistance makes us unhappy. It takes us out of the moment. The mind cannot accept, so when you are in the mind, you suffer. When you go out of the mind, when you aren't thinking so heavily, then the acceptance comes. And acceptance is amazing. Acceptance takes the resistance away. Then you relax. You let go. You go to ecstasy, and you experience the higher being.

So when resistance is gone, we have fun with whatever goes on. Hey a poetry! Acceptance takes the resistance away and all of a sudden joy comes. Joy means no resistance.